THE
KITCHEN SINK
COOKBOOK

Also by Carolyn Wyman

I'm a Spam Fan

THE

KITCHEN SINK

COOKBOOK

Offbeat Recipes From Unusual Ingredients

Carolyn Wyman

A Birch Lane Press Book
Published by Carol Publishing Group

A Birch Lane Press Book
Published by Carol Publishing Group
Birch Lane Press is a registered trademark of Carol Communications, Inc.

Editorial, sales and distribution, and rights and permissions inquiries should be addressed to Carol Publishing Group, 120 Enterprise Avenue, Secaucus, N.J. 07094.

In Canada: Canadian Manda Group, One Atlantic Avenue, Suite 105, Toronto, Ontario M6K 3E7

Carol Publishing Group books may be purchased in bulk at special discounts for sales promotion, fund-raising, or educational purposes. Special editions can be created to specifications. For details, contact Special Sales Department, Carol Publishing Group, 120 Enterprise Avenue, Secaucus, N.J. 07094.

Designed by Jessica Shatan

Manufactured in the United States of America
10 9 8 7 6 5 4 3 2 1

Library of Congress Cataloging-in-Publication Data

Wyman, Carolyn.
    The kitchen sink cookbook : offbeat recipes from unusual
ingredients / Carolyn Wyman.
        p.   cm.
    "A Birch Lane Press book."
    ISBN 1-55972-405-6 (hc)
    1. Cookery.   2. Cookery—Humor.   I. Title.
TX714.W94   1997
641.5—dc21   97–585
                                                                      CIP

For Harold Austin (1911–1978), truly a great uncle

The recipes and suggestions in this book were compiled from a variety of sources. While they are all intended to be used, the author and publisher do not take, or do they assume, any responsibility for their safety or deliciousness. Particular care should be taken with recipes involving edible flowers and plants, flaming, and machines not normally used in the preparation of foods.

A number of products mentioned in this book are trademarks. Unless otherwise indicated, the companies that own these trademarks have not supplied nor do they endorse the recipes or suggestions in this book. For a full listing of trademark owners, see page 188.

Grateful acknowledgment is made for permission to reprint the following recipes:

Mt. Nebo Mock Lobster Salad (here called Mock Lobster Salad) from *Sinkin Spells, Hot Flashes, Fits and Cravins,* copyright 1988 by Ernest Matthew Mickler, with permission from Ten Speed Press, P.O. Box 7123, Berkeley, CA 94707.

Handcream Dip excerpted from *Giga Bites: The Hacker Cookbook,* copyright 1994 by Jenz Johnson, with permission from Ten Speed Press, P.O. Box 7123, Berkeley, CA 94707.

Contents

3 Fashions and Obsessions 49

4 Flora and Fauna 76

5 Special Effects 97

9 Ready-to-Eat 173

Listing of Recipes by Category

Breakfast or Brunch

Breakfast Bowl Volcano
Breakfast in the Bag
Blooming Fun Breakfast Eggs
Continental Breakfast in an
    Orange
Corncob Jelly
Drunken Mammy Pancakes
Earthworm Omelet
Hot Rice Breakfast Cereal
Mashed Potato Doughnuts
Pancakes Canned Corn
Pollen Pancakes
Scrapple
Stewed Pretzels

Appetizers and Snacks

Edible Paper Art
Frankly Weird Hors D'Oeuvre
Granola Fondue
Handcream Dip
Hoppers à la Provençe
Mock Fried Mushrooms
Nachos Casserole a Go-Go
Pig Newtons
Pooch Pâté

Salads

All-Orange Salad
BBQ Jell-O
Beer Cole Slaw

"Can"-You-Really-Be-That-Old
    Birthday Casserole
Chicken With Chocolate and Chilies
    (Chicken Mole)
Chicken With 101 Cloves of Garlic
Coca-Cola BBQ Chicken
Black-Eyed Pea Guaca-Jell-O-Salad
Mock Lobster Salad
Squid Salad
Stinging Nettle Salad Unplugged
Strawberry Surprise Salad
The World's Easiest Rice (or Pasta)
    Salad
Four-Legged Turkey
Pretzel Chicken
7-Up Glazed Duck
Tea Bag–Stuffed Chicken
Truly Dressed Turkey
Watermelon-Baked Chicken

Fish
Baby Shrimp on Pasta
Cat Kebabs
Clothes Dryer Shrimp
Floundering Towards Florida
Grilled Eel
7-Up Batter Fish

Salmon Dirty Dishes
Sushi

Other Entrées
Alligator Steak
Blood Pudding
French Cream Pizza
Mock Goose
Movie Theater Lobby Loaf
Noodles Nasturtium
Spud Pizza
Thanksgiving Stuffed Pumpkin
Turtle Kebabs
White Castle Lasagne

Cakes
Checkerboard Cake
Chocolate Mayonnaise Cake
Classic Tomato Soup Cake
Dessert Burgers
Frigid Wedding Cake
Ice Cream and Cake Mix-Up
Jell-O Poke Cake
Jerky Cake
Kitty Litter Cake
Metamorphosis Dessert
Old Glory Cake
Rabbit Hole Cake

Red Velvet Cake
Sauerkraut Surprise Cake
Self-Frosting Cake
Size 9W Cake
Southern Belle In-A-Cake
Spider Cake

Cookies
All-Washed-Up Oatmeal Cookies
Castor Oil Cookies
Dog Bone Treats
Giant Cookie
Half-Baked Cookies
Potato Chip Cookies
Sprout Chip Cookies

Pies
Astronaut Pie
Mock Coconut Pie
Piecrust of Champions
Popcorn Pie
Ritz Mock Apple Pie
Southern Insect Pie
Vinegar Pie

Candy
Chocolate Pinto Beans
Chow Mein Candy

Dessert Domes
Flower Candy
No. 2 Yellow Candy Pencils
Spud Fudge
Velveeta Fudge

Ice Cream and Frozen Desserts
Avocado Ice Cream
Beer Sorbet
Garlic Ice Cream
Fire and Ice
Ice Cream Cold Feet
Ice Cream Sunny-side Up
Prune Ice Cream
Red Beans and Sweet Corn Frozen
    Delight
Sugar on Snow
Tabasco Ice Cream

Puddings and Gelatin
Beet Pudding
Black Jell-O
By the Sea
Clover Custard
Cracker Pudding
Dirt Dessert
Doughnut Pudding

Acknowledgments

Even books with a premise as fun as this one involve heapin' helpin's of work. I was fortunate to have a lot of help in doing it.

In addition to the companies and organizations mentioned in the headnotes of particular recipes or acknowledged in the permissions or trademark pages, I am grateful to have received recipes or research help from Philip Greenvall, James "Dad" Wyman, Linda Tillson, Jean Walton, Katherine J. Rodgers, Marilyn Buel, Mark Lambeck, Teresa Gubbins, Valerie Kraemer, Bill and Susan Halldin, Mary Thies, Lee Bellows, Robert Wildman, Patrick Dilger, Marc Abrahams, Theresa Aragao, Dave Byers, John David Auwen, Ray Bruman, Gudrun Achtenhagen, Donald Dandelski, Jan Longone of the Wine and Food Library of Ann Arbor, Michigan, Nach Waxman of Kitchen Arts & Letters in New York City, the staffs of the Russell, New Haven, Killingly, and Madison, Connecticut, public libraries, and the intrepid Pack-Solomon family (intrepid because they agreed to taste-test some recipes in this book even after learning of its subtitle).

I'm also indebted to Jim Ellison and Lisa Kaufman of Carol Publishing for recognizing the potential of this idea and for helping me to shape the idea into something both readable and edible.

Special thanks are also due Phil Blumenkrantz and Joyce Morral for counsel on the relative weirdness of various recipes, and for themselves being so wonderfully offbeat that their judgment on such matters could not be questioned. They, and Philip Greenvall, also shouldered the bulk of my whining during the writing.

As for the friends, family, and newspaper colleagues who lent support by giving me space: Now that the work is over, you're all invited over for Moose Meatballs.

Introduction

Most people will tell you that food should taste good, look good, and be good for you. But in an age when food that fits all three of these criteria is only a restaurant or supermarket deli and a few bucks away, I say recipes worth the trouble of home cooking had better do more than that.

Specifically I think they should be as entertaining as *Star Wars,* as attention-arresting as an unexpected IRS notice—should, in fact, at least at times, cause stomachs to churn and people to gasp, or laugh, or cry. At least, that's my hope for the recipes in this book.

Getting that kind of rise out of people today is admittedly not as easy as it used to be. That's because America is weirder and more open to weirdness than it used to be, especially when it comes to food. Increased acceptance of ethnic cuisine means that Thai peanut butter dipping sauce, barbecue chicken pizza, and break-fast burritos have become almost as American as hamburgers and apple pie. Cereals based on desserts and candy bars have become common and the one based on Rice Krispies Treats so popular that manufacturer Kellogg's took out advertisements apologizing for shortages. A few months later, a major national TV dinner maker came out with a line of organic vegan Italian dinners in which tofu replaces cheese. If this is mainstream American eating in the 90s, then what's offbeat?

It's a very subjective thing, obviously, which means my choices here will be subject to lots of questioning and criticism. If you have a recipe you think is as weird or weirder than anything here, please send it along to me care of Carol Publishing, 120 Enterprise Ave., Secaucus, N.J. 07094 and if it's not just some inedible joke, I may end up using it in some future edition of this book.

What you'll find between these covers at the moment are recipes reflecting a definition of weird broad enough to include foods with unexpected or hidden ingredients; foods that are part of unfamiliar ethnic, historic, or geographic traditions; foods made from little-known or used ingredients; foods that defy convention in their preparation or cooking; foods that double as art; and foods that have purposes beyond repast.

People who are familiar with my syndicated food column ("Supermarket Sampler") and previous food book *I'm a Spam Fan* will probably be relieved to hear that very few of the recipes in this collection are of my own creation. Most were inspired by or reprinted from food histories, community cookbooks, international cookbooks, single subject cookbooks, restaurant menus, food contest entries, or booklets from trade associations and food manufacturers—in other words, people and organizations who know and love their favorite foodstuff so much that they have completely lost sight of normal limits surrounding its use. From such boundary busting comes both greatness and craziness.

Whether great or crazy or a little bit of both, all these recipes were meant to be made. These recipes would have been weirder—and this book much easier to write—if they were not. But then this would be a joke book and not the cookbook-that-doesn't-take-itself-too-seriously that it was meant to be.

This is not to say that all these recipes taste great—only that the ones that do not taste great are worth making for some other good reason, like their good looks or what they do, or the big "Oooooh" you'll get out of guests when you serve them.

Any old food will take away hunger pains. The food in this book will feed your hunger and quench your thirst for fun.

THE
KITCHEN SINK
COOKBOOK

1

SECRET INGREDIENTS

We all love secrets. How else to explain the popularity of murder mysteries, the allure of a locked diary, the appeal of an after-dinner guessing game?

But why wait until after dinner when you can serve food that provides nourishment and an element of surprise all at the same time?

I do not mean the kind of culinary surprise you get when you discover that your teenage son ate the slice of meatloaf that was going to be your lunch. Nor are we referring to the mystery of faithfully following a recipe for a loaf of bread that turns out more like a block of cinder. No, a thousand times no.

Instead, what I mean to subject you to in this chapter are foods that taste good but not at all like you might expect, given what's in them. Foods that challenge your sensory experience and taste prejudices. Foods that undergo some kind of chemical taste change when cooked in combination with other ingredients. Foods that, when served to the adventurous, cry out to be introduced with the challenge, "I'll bet you can't guess what's in this," or, to the timid, with the warning, "Don't ask. You don't want to know."

BEEF À LA CAFFEINE

In the past few years Americans have gone crazy for good coffee. How else to explain why those new coffeehouses and bars are such a success? I know it's not because anyone loves balancing on those spindly black stools or losing our fillings to those $4 petrified-wood cookies sold as accompaniments.

Anyway, true coffee addicts also love coffee-flavored foods. Cappuccino muffins and espresso-flavored ice cream are good but we were thinking of something a bit more substantial—like this beef dish developed by the Brazilian Coffee Institute.

You can't really taste the coffee in the sauce it helps to make, but caffeine fiends should find its presence both a kick and a comfort—not to mention a happy alternative to the crime of pouring $2.50-a-cup leftovers down the sink.

¼ cup (½ stick) salted butter	*¾ cup dry white wine*
2 pounds cubed beef	*2 teaspoons salt*
1 garlic clove, crushed	*½ teaspoon oregano*
3 onions, sliced	*1 cup strong coffee*
¼ cup all-purpose flour	*Hot cooked rice*

In a deep skillet, melt the butter and brown the meat. Sauté the garlic and onions in the same pan with the meat. Remove the meat, garlic, and onions from the skillet. Mix the flour with the remaining butter in skillet. Add the wine, salt, oregano, and coffee. Cook, stirring until slightly thickened.

Return the meat, garlic, and onions to the skillet. Cover and bring to a boil. Lower the heat and cook slowly for 1½ hours, or until the meat is tender. Serve over hot cooked rice. *6 servings.*

MASHED POTATO DOUGHNUTS

Okay, so this isn't the easiest recipe in the world. But it'll all be worth it when you bite into these for the first time—the texture's as terrific as the fun of telling people what they're made of.

Still not convinced? Then maybe this spud's NOT for you.

3 tablespoons solid vegetable
  shortening
¾ cup sugar, plus additional sugar
  for dipping
3 large eggs, beaten
⅓ cup milk
2¾ cups all-purpose flour

4 teaspoons baking powder
1 teaspoon salt
1 teaspoon cinnamon
½ teaspoon grated nutmeg
½ teaspoon ground cloves
1 cup mashed potatoes
Vegetable oil for frying

Add the shortening and sugar to the beaten eggs and beat again. Add the milk, flour, baking powder, salt, cinnamon, nutmeg, and cloves and mix until well blended. Then blend in the mashed potatoes. Refrigerate the dough, then go watch TV for 2 to 3 hours.

Separate the dough into 3 pieces. Roll each third out to a ⅓-inch thickness on a floured board. Cut into 3-inch circles with a cookie cutter or inverted glass and lightly flour. Fry in deep fat heated to 375° F until golden brown, turning once in about a minute, or as soon as the doughnuts rise.

Drain on paper towels and dip in granulated sugar. *Makes about 35 doughnuts.*

BLACK-EYED PEA BOLOGNA

Most people eat black-eyed peas plain or with ham hocks. But the "reci-pea" contest of Athens, Texas's annual July Black-Eyed Pea Jamboree has produced some far more interesting ways to stare down that region's most plentiful legume. Would you believe black-eyed pea meatballs, candy, cookies, and, my favorite, this hamburger-black-eyed pea all-purpose amalgam?

It won a richly deserved third place for creators Kellie and Darlene Deupree in 1982.

2 pounds ground chuck
2 tablespoons salt
½ teaspoon garlic powder
1 teaspoon mustard seed

1 tablespoon liquid smoke
1 teaspoon onion powder
1 teaspoon cracked black pepper
2 15.5 ounce cans black-eyed peas

Mix all the ingredients together with your hands. Shape into 3 rolls about 2 inches in diameter. Wrap each roll in plastic wrap, tying the ends tight with twist wires. Refrigerate for 24 hours.

Preheat the oven to 300°F. Remove the plastic wrap and put rolls on an oven rack with a pan below to catch any drippings. Bake 1½ hours. Wrap in foil and refrigerate. Slice and serve with eggs for breakfast, on pizza and sandwiches, or anywhere you would use meat. *8 to 10 servings.*

BURGER DESSERT SQUARES

Yes, you read it right: these are dessert bars whose primary ingredient is two pounds of ground beef. Burger Dessert Squares are actually only one of about half a dozen recipes in common circulation for dense fruit and/or nut cakes or desserts that also feature beef, pork, sausage—even Spam.

If you're shocked, then you've probably never heard of mincemeat, or have forgotten what it was originally made of: minced beef and beef suet—along with the chopped fruits, nuts, spices, and spirits that are the only ingredients of today's commercially prepared mincemeat products.

Constance Beckwith was doubtless thinking of mincemeat when she created this 1981 National Beef Cook-Off prizewinning dish which she called Sweet Meat Bars.

2 pounds lean ground beef
1 16-ounce can whole berry
   cranberry sauce
1½ cups packed dark brown sugar
1 cup raisins
¾ cup coarsely chopped walnuts
½ cup orange marmalade
½ cup orange juice

2 tablespoons grated fresh orange
   peel
3 teaspoons salt, divided
4 cups all-purpose flour
2 tablespoons baking powder
1⅓ cups plus 3 tablespoons milk
⅔ cup vegetable oil
1½ cups confectioners' sugar
1 tablespoon rum

Preheat the oven to 425° F.

Place the ground beef, cranberry sauce, brown sugar, raisins, walnuts, orange marmalade, orange juice, orange peel, and 1 teaspoon salt in a Dutch oven. Cook over medium heat until the mixture boils. Lower the heat and continue cooking 20 minutes, stirring constantly. Cool.

Meanwhile, combine the flour, baking powder, and remaining 2 teaspoons salt; add 1⅓ cups milk and oil all at once, stirring until the flour is moistened.

Place the dough on wax paper and knead about 10 times; divide in half. Roll half the dough between 2 sheets of wax paper to fit a 17 x 10-inch jelly roll pan. Peel off the top sheet of wax paper and invert the dough onto a jelly roll pan.

Carefully peel off other piece of wax paper; press the dough to fit over the bottom and up the sides of the pan. Spoon the cooled beef mixture over the dough. Roll the second half of dough into a 17 x 10-inch rectangle. Remove the top sheet of wax paper and invert the dough over the beef mixture. Remove the second sheet of wax paper. Press the edges of the dough together to seal. Make 4 slashes in the top crust.

Bake 25 to 30 minutes, or until the crust is golden brown. Meanwhile, combine the confectioners' sugar, 3 tablespoons milk and the rum to make a glaze; mix until smooth. Let the dessert cool slightly and drizzle with glaze, then cut into bars. *Makes 24 bars.*

POOCH PÂTÉ

We've all heard how the depression-era poor sometimes ate dog food. When I called the Heinz Cycle Dog Food 800 help line to ask about the wisdom of doing this today, the friendly woman on the other end explained that there is hardly a baby in America that hasn't eaten dog food at one time or another and look at how many of us are still walking around today.

While not designed to please human palates of any age, I'd venture to say that the flavored gourmet dog and cat foods of today taste a whole lot better than the stuff stock market victims were wolfing down in the thirties. In fact, some people say they taste like pâté.

1 3-ounce can chicken-flavored
non-chunky dog or cat food
1½ tablespoons mayonnaise

Seasonings (such as garlic powder,
red pepper, parsley and/or
seasoned salt) to taste
Crackers

Mix together the dog or cat food, mayonnaise, and seasonings and serve on crackers. *Serves 4 to 6 people if they don't know what they're eating; at least twice as many if they do.*

ALTERNATIVE VERSION FOR THE LAWSUIT-WARY: Substitute a 2½-ounce jar of beef baby food for the pet food.

BABY SHRIMP ON PASTA

We all know of adults who act like babies, so perhaps it should not be surprising to learn that a fair number of adults eat baby food. At least some eat it in cooking, the most common substitution being baby food carrots in place of ones that have to be peeled and grated in carrot cake recipes. Less common are the people who use baby formula to help them make white sauce.

But considering that this recipe of Helen Danhof's won first prize in the National Baby Food Festival Cook-Off in baby food maker Gerber's hometown of Fremont, Michigan, in 1994, and that the first prize winner in 1995 also used formula, I would imagine it is not going to seem like a strange idea for very long.

2 pounds shrimp	2 tablespoons cornstarch
1 pound thin spaghetti	1/4 cup chopped fresh parsley
1/2 cup (1 stick) salted butter or olive oil	2 teaspoons chopped chives
2 garlic cloves, minced	Salt and pepper to taste
1 13-ounce can Gerber Baby Formula concentrated liquid (do not add water)	

Peel and devein the shrimp. Cook and drain the spaghetti. In a heavy skillet, melt the butter, add the shrimp and garlic, and cook for 4 minutes over medium heat, stirring. With a slotted spoon, remove the shrimp and set aside.

Slowly add the baby formula and bring to a boil. Mix the cornstarch with 4 tablespoons water and add to the formula. Stir until thickened.

Add the shrimp, parsley, chives, and salt and pepper, stirring until well blended. Serve over the cooked spaghetti. This dish goes well with Gerber Graduate peas. *4 to 6 servings.*

CLASSIC TOMATO SOUP CAKE

No less a culinary personage than M.F.K. Fisher gave this moist, reddish spice cake her blessing: one, because it keeps well; two, because it will unfussily bake in a moderate oven filled with other things; three, for the fun of quizzing people about its key ingredient.

Considering how long Classic Tomato Soup Cake has been around (since 1925, according to recipe supplier Campbell), perhaps what's most surprising is the number of people who are still surprised by it.

2 cups all-purpose flour
1⅓ cups sugar
4 teaspoons baking powder
1 teaspoon baking soda
1½ teaspoons ground allspice
1 teaspoon cinnamon

½ teaspoon ground cloves
1 10¾-ounce can Campbell's
    Condensed Tomato Soup
½ cup solid vegetable shortening
2 large eggs

Preheat the oven to 350°F. Grease and flour 2 8-inch round cake pans.

In a large bowl, combine all the ingredients with ¼ cup water. With the mixer at low speed, beat until well mixed, constantly scraping the bowl with a rubber spatula. Beat 4 minutes at high speed, occasionally scraping the bowl. Pour into the prepared pans.

Bake 35 to 40 minutes, or until a toothpick inserted in the center comes out clean. Cool in the pans on wire racks 10 minutes. Remove from the pans; cool completely. Frost with canned or homemade cream cheese frosting, if desired. *12 servings.*

CHOCOLATE MAYONNAISE CAKE

The blue ribbon on the Hellmann's Mayonnaise jar is not there in commemoration of some long-ago food prize. It's there because of the way New York deli owner Richard Hellmann first began selling his mayonnaise: as a to-go item out of two big glass jars he decorated with blue ribbons.

As for his beloved recipe for Chocolate Mayonnaise Cake: it was actually invented by Mrs. Paul Prince, the wife of one of the Hellmann's company's sales distributors in 1937, or about twenty-two years after manufacturing mayonnaise had become Hellmann's only business.

Her original recipe was dense like a brownie and contained walnuts and dates but no eggs. The company's current version has neither walnuts and dates and is lighter in texture. But the mayonnaise still makes the cake magically moist and tender without revealing its own taste.

2 cups unsifted all-purpose flour (or
*   2¼ cups unsifted cake flour)*
⅔ cup unsweetened cocoa
1¼ teaspoons baking soda
¼ teaspoon baking powder
3 large eggs

1⅔ cups sugar
1 teaspoon vanilla extract
1 cup Hellmann's or Best Foods real or
*   light mayonnaise or low-fat*
*   mayonnaise dressing*

Preheat the oven to 350°F. Grease and flour the bottom of 2 9-inch round cake pans.

In a medium bowl, combine the flour, cocoa, baking soda, and baking powder; set aside.

In a large bowl with the mixer at high speed, beat the eggs, sugar, and vanilla 3 minutes, or until light and fluffy. Reduce the speed to low; beat in the mayonnaise until blended. Add the flour mixture in 4 additions, alternately with 1⅓ cups water (beginning and ending with flour). Pour into the prepared pans.

Bake 30 to 35 minutes, or until a toothpick inserted in the center comes out clean. Cool in the pans on wire racks 10 minutes. Remove; cool completely on racks. Frost as desired. *Makes 1 9-inch layer cake.*

SAUERKRAUT SURPRISE CAKE

Classic Tomato Soup Cake and Chocolate Mayonnaise Cake were both inventions of tomato soup and mayonnaise makers who wanted to give people more reasons to buy their products.

The origins of the third of the mystery ingredient cake triumvirate is more mysterious. As far as we know, there is no sauerkraut manufacturer claiming credit (or blame); no folk tale of the cook carrying sauerkraut who tripped so that the fermented vegetable fell into the cake batter. And it's hard to imagine anyone just deciding to try this out of the clear blue.

People say sauerkraut's effect on cake is similar to coconut but if that was the intention, why didn't the inventor just use coconut?

I don't know. But if they had, this recipe (from the industry group Pickle Packers International) wouldn't have been half as interesting.

⅔ cup margarine or salted butter
1½ cups sugar
3 large eggs
1 teaspoon vanilla extract
½ cup unsweetened cocoa
2¼ cups sifted all-purpose flour

1 teaspoon baking powder
1 teaspoon baking soda
¼ teaspoon salt
⅔ cup (a little less than an 8-ounce can) sauerkraut, rinsed, drained, and chopped

SOUR CREAM ICING

1 6-ounce package semisweet
   chocolate chips
4 tablespoons ($\frac{1}{2}$ stick) salted butter

$\frac{1}{2}$ cup sour cream
1 teaspoon vanilla extract
$\frac{1}{4}$ teaspoon salt
$2\frac{1}{2}$ to $2\frac{3}{4}$ cups confectioners' sugar

Preheat the oven to 350°F. Grease and flour 2 8-inch square or round baking pans.

Thoroughly cream the margarine with the sugar. Beat in the eggs and vanilla. Sift together the cocoa, flour, baking powder, baking soda, and salt; add the dry mixture alternately with 1 cup water to the egg mixture. Stir in the sauerkraut.

Spoon into the prepared baking pans. Bake about 30 to 35 minutes, or until a wooden pick inserted in the center comes out clean and the cake begins to pull away from the sides of the pan. Let cool. Frost with whipped cream or Sour Cream Icing.

To make the icing: Melt the chocolate chips with the butter, then blend in the sour cream, vanilla and salt. Add confectioners' sugar in stages until the frosting is of spreading consistency. Then beat well. *Makes 1 8-inch layer cake.*

HERSHEY'S COCOA CHILI

You might think the International Chili Society would be the best source for unusual chili recipes. But you would be wrong. That group has all sorts of rules as to what people can put into their chili to keep the competition fair—and the chili fairly uniform and uninteresting.

One allowed exception is the Dutch cocoa or unsweetened chocolate some chili chefs use to smooth out the harsh taste of chili powders.

Although cocoa may seem unusual in a meat dish, it has a heritage in the mole sauces of Mexico (see Chapter 2) and a booster in cocoa maker and recipe provider Hershey.

1 28-ounce can or 3½ cups whole
   tomatoes, undrained and cut up
½ cup tomato juice
5 tablespoons vegetable shortening
4 pounds coarsely ground lean beef
2 cups coarsely chopped onion
2 garlic cloves, minced
4 bay leaves
4 tablespoons chili powder

3 tablespoons Hershey's Cocoa
2 teaspoons oregano
2 teaspoons ground cumin
2 teaspoons sugar
1½ to 2 teaspoons salt
½ teaspoon cayenne
2 tablespoons chopped fresh cilantro
4 to 5 tablespoons all-purpose flour

In 2-gallon saucepan or kettle, combine 4 cups water, the tomatoes, and tomato juice; begin cooking over medium heat.

Meanwhile, in a skillet, melt the shortening; add the beef and chopped onion. Cook, stirring occasionally, until browned; immediately add the beef and onion to the tomato mixture. Add the garlic, bay leaves, chili powder, cocoa, oregano, cumin, sugar, salt, and cayenne. Heat to boiling.

Reduce the heat; simmer 2½ to 3 hours. Add additional water if the chili gets too thick during cooking. About 30 minutes before the chili is done, add the cilantro. Mix the flour with ⅓ cup cold water; add to the chili.

Continue to cook, stirring constantly, until the chili is thickened. *Makes about 3 to 4 quarts chili.*

STRAWBERRY SURPRISE SALAD

Are Jell-O salads meant to be eaten as salads or as desserts? The answer, of course, is both. As to when this particular Jell-O salad should be served, opinion is divided. But the greater question is: what is this crust's primary ingredient?

After finding out about the pretzels, many will assume this recipe was born of the recent widespread fear of fat and the pretzel's rediscovery as a low-fat snack. But Strawberry Surprise Salad has actually been making bridge club rounds since the 1960s.

2 cups pretzels
¾ cup (1½ sticks) salted butter
1 8-ounce package cream cheese, softened at room temperature
½ cup sugar
1 8-ounce container Cool Whip, defrosted
1 3-ounce box strawberry Jell-O
1 3-ounce box raspberry Jell-O
1 16-ounce package frozen strawberries, thawed
1 8-ounce can crushed pineapple and juice

Preheat the oven to 400°F.

Crush the pretzels with a rolling pin. Melt the butter and mix with the pretzels. Spread in the bottom of a 9 x 13-inch pan or oven dish. Bake 7 minutes, then set aside to cool.

Beat together the softened cream cheese and sugar, then gradually fold in the Cool Whip. Spread on the crust so that it is totally covered, then place the pan in the refrigerator.

Dissolve the contents of the 2 Jell-O boxes in 2 cups boiling water and stir in the strawberries and pineapple. Chill until slightly jelled (about an hour), then pour the Jell-O mixture over the cream cheese filling.

Return the pan to the refrigerator for several hours or until completely set. *8 servings.*

NOTE FOR NUTRITIONAL SCAREDY-CATS: This recipe also works with light cream cheese and Cool Whip Lite.

CHOW MEIN CANDY

The longest and most engaging conversation at a potluck holiday party I attended a few years back consisted of people trying to guess the main ingredient in this crunchy chocolate peanut butter candy. What's more, this showstopper probably took about an eighth the time and effort to create than anything else on the table.

Successful alternative versions can be made using butterscotch chips, cocktail peanuts or peanut butter in place of the peanut butter chips and cans of shoestring potato sticks instead of the noodles.

1 12-ounce package semisweet chocolate chips

1 12-ounce package peanut butter morsels

1 3-ounce can chow mein noodles

Empty the chocolate chips and peanut butter morsels into a microwave-safe bowl and microwave on low to medium heat, stopping to stir occasionally, until melted. (Be careful not to overcook!) Immediately add the chow mein noodles and stir with a spoon until they are completely coated. Drop onto wax paper with a tablespoon. Let cool until firm. *Makes about 3 dozen.*

FRANKLY WEIRD HORS D'OEUVRE

Although I have forgotten almost everything I learned in high school algebra and French classes, I still remember this cocktail frank hors d'oeuvre a neighbor served to my family about this same time.

I have since encountered alternative versions using red currant instead of grape jelly and a jar of shrimp cocktail sauce or chili sauce instead of the mustard. All are equally delicious and unlikely.

1 10-ounce jar grape jelly	2 5-ounce cans Vienna sausages or
1 8-ounce jar spicy brown mustard	equivalent amount of cocktail
	weiners

In a medium-sized saucepan over medium heat, cook the grape jelly and mustard and stir until the jelly dissolves. Transfer to a chafing dish and add the cocktail weiners.

Serve warm with toothpicks as an appetizer. *4 servings.*

NOTE: Sliced hot dogs can be used in place of the Vienna sausages or cocktail franks.

THE WORLD'S EASIEST RICE (OR PASTA) SALAD

The new generation of premium TV dinner entrées are quite delicious. In fact, I would venture to say that few home chefs cook as well as the professional food scientists at Stouffer's. The question is: Are you mature enough to admit this to yourself and does your kitchen trash can have a cover so you can hide it from everyone else?

If so, then you should definitely try this delicious, incredibly easy, timesaving recipe. Buy your entrées with coupons or during a sale and this dish could also cost as little as $1 per serving.

6 packages of any one of your favorite rice or pasta-based frozen entrée (such as Budget Gourmet Slim Selects Penne Pasta, or Chinese or Italian Style Vegetables and Chicken)

Cook the entrées in the microwave according to package directions, allowing for enough time to cook only 1 or 2 at a time, depending on your microwave size. Empty the packages into 1 large serving bowl. Refrigerate until just before eating. *6 to 8 servings.*

12–TEA BAG SOUP

One of my favorite cookbooks of 1996 is a fascinating if somewhat self-serving guide to using herbal teas as much as humanly possible by Celestial Seasonings tea company founders Jennifer and Mo Siegel. The focus of *Celestial Seasonings Cooking With Tea* is, as the title suggests, on using tea bags in marinades, salad dressings, soups, and sauces as a time- and brain-saver over having to figure out and measure out spices.

The following is my adaptation of a Siegel soup recipe using an impressive half a box of Celestial Seasonings tea.

1 4- to 5-pound chicken
12 Celestial Seasonings Sleepytime tea bags
5 carrots, chopped
2 onions, peeled and chopped

2 turnips, peeled and chopped
3 celery stalks, chopped
1 cup rice (any kind)
Salt and pepper

Put the chicken and 7 quarts water in a large stockpot. Bring to a boil over high heat, then reduce the heat to low and simmer, partially covered, for about 2 hours, or until the chicken is done. (Check the white meat after an hour and remove it if it's done so it doesn't get tough.) Skim off any scum that collects on the top as it cooks.

Remove the chicken from the pot and when it has cooled, pick the meat off the bones and cut into bite-sized pieces.

Add the tea bags to the cleaned-off broth, bring to a boil for 7 minutes, then remove and discard the bags. Add the carrots, onions, turnips, celery, and rice. Season with salt and pepper. Simmer on low heat for an additional 1½ hours. Add as much or as little chicken as desired and continue cooking another 15 to 30 minutes. *30 servings.*

POTATO CHIP COOKIES

Can't decide whether to have a salty or a sweet snack? You don't have to if you make a batch of these surprisingly excellent sugar cookies with crushed potato chips, inspired by a Snack Food Association recipe.

½ cup (1 stick) salted butter
½ cup granulated sugar
½ cup light brown sugar
1 egg, well beaten

1 cup all-purpose flour
½ teaspoon baking soda
1 teaspoon vanilla extract
½ cup finely crushed potato chips

Preheat the oven to 350°F.

Cream the butter and sugars together until smooth. Add the egg. Slowly mix in the flour and baking soda, making sure no lumps form. Stir in the vanilla and potato chips. Drop by teaspoonfuls onto ungreased baking sheet 2 inches apart and bake 9 to 12 minutes. *Makes about 2 dozen cookies.*

COCA-COLA BBQ CHICKEN

Soda pop is as much a staple of American kitchens as wine is in French ones. That's probably why community cookbooks in America are bubbling over with recipes for soda-infused cakes, roasts, salads, and sauces and French cookbooks sport recipes for coq au vin, beef burgundy, and steak Bordelaise.

Coca-Cola is America's best-selling soft drink and also, not surprisingly, its favorite soda pop to cook with. In fact, many soda pop chefs swear by Coca-Cola Classic exclusively—saying that Pepsi is too sweet and that any diet soft drink will leave a bitter aftertaste.

Combine Coca-Cola Classic with ketchup as instructed in this official company chicken casserole recipe, though, and you'll end with something that tastes for all the world like slow-cooked barbecue chicken.

3 pounds cut-up chicken or chicken
   breasts, thighs, and legs
⅓ cup all-purpose flour
5 teaspoons salt
⅓ cup vegetable oil
½ cup finely diced onion
½ cup finely diced celery
½ cup finely diced green pepper

1 cup ketchup
1 cup Coca-Cola Classic
2 tablespoons Worcestershire sauce
½ teaspoon hickory smoked salt
½ teaspoon dried basil leaves
½ teaspoon chili powder
⅛ teaspoon pepper
Hot cooked rice for serving

Preheat the oven to 350° F.

Rinse the chicken pieces; pat dry. Coat the chicken with the flour mixed with 2 teaspoons salt. Heat the oil in a large skillet and brown the chicken pieces on all sides, then place the pieces in a 3-quart casserole. (Discard the drippings.) Combine the remaining ingredients except rice, mixing well. Spoon the sauce over the chicken, covering all the pieces. Cover the casserole and bake about 1¼ hours, or until the chicken is fork-tender. If desired, serve the chicken with sauce on hot cooked rice. *4 to 6 servings.*

UNENDORSED STOVE-TOP VERSION FOR LAZY PERSONS: Put some cut-up chicken parts in a large covered skillet, douse with equal amounts of Coca-Cola and ketchup, and cook over medium heat until the sauce is thickened and the chicken is fork-tender.

7-UP BATTER FISH

Surely you've heard of beer batter fish. Well, 7-Up works equally well for the same purpose. Its ephemeral bubbles somehow seem to live on in an incredibly light, fluffy, and crunchy batter.

2 cups Bisquick or other buttermilk biscuit mix	1 egg, slightly beaten
1¼ cups 7-Up	Vegetable oil
	3 pounds sole, cod or haddock fillets

Put the Bisquick, 7-Up, and egg in a shallow dish and mix thoroughly. Dip the fish in the batter and coat both sides well.

In a Dutch oven heat the oil to 350°F. Add the fish and fry 1 to 2 minutes a side, or until golden brown. The fish should flake easily with a fork. *4 servings.*

7-UP GLAZED DUCK

The nutritional naughtiness of cooking with soda becomes even more appealing when the soda is used to prepare a gourmet dish like duck. Versions of this recipe appear in several 7-Up company cookbooks as well as in countless community and church ones.

1 4- to 5-pound duckling	1 teaspoon caraway seeds
Salt and pepper	¼ teaspoon salt
⅓ cup dark brown sugar	1 7-ounce bottle 7-Up
2 teaspoons cornstarch	1 cup halved seedless white grapes

Preheat the oven to 325° F.

Remove the fat from the duck cavity; cut off the extra neck skin. Season with the salt and pepper. Place the duck on a roasting pan, skin side down, and bake.

Meanwhile, mix the brown sugar, cornstarch, caraway seeds, and salt in a saucepan. Stir in 7-Up and cook over low heat, stirring until slightly thickened. Then add the grapes and cook until the sauce is thickened.

After the duck has baked for 2 hours, brush some sauce on it, leaving the rest in the saucepan. Bake an additional 30 minutes to an hour, or until the duck is tender. Spoon the remaining sauce on the duck as it is served. *4 to 6 servings.*

DRUNKEN MAMMY PANCAKES

Soda and beer are kissin' cousins when it comes to cooking. That's what made us think of substituting beer for soda pop in a pancake recipe we found. That, and the morning-after cure that calls for a hair of the dog! The beer makes for a hearty-tasting crepelike pancake.

1 cup pancake mix, such as Aunt Jemima
½ to 1 cup beer (whatever amount of liquid the box cooking instructions specify)

1 egg, slightly beaten
1 to 2 tablespoons vegetable oil
¼ teaspoon ground cinnamon

Combine all the ingredients; mix until smooth. Spoon three pools of batter onto a lightly greased griddle and cook until the tops of the pancakes are covered with bubbles. Turn over and cook 2 to 3 minutes more, or until light brown. *Makes about 12 to 16 pancakes.*

BEER COLE SLAW

Some people (obviously of narrow vision) see beer in cole slaw and say why. We say, why not?

1 medium head cabbage
1 small red onion
2 carrots, peeled
1 cup mayonnaise

1 7-ounce bottle of beer (sissy size)
½ cup raisins
2 teaspoons celery seeds (optional)

Grate or chop the cabbage, onion, and carrots and place in a large bowl.

In a separate bowl, mix together the mayonnaise, beer, raisins, and celery seeds. Blend well. Pour the dressing over the vegetables and mix everything together until all the veggies are coated.

Refrigerate. *4 servings.*

PRUNE BROWNIES

Want to see how much America has changed? Look at our brownie recipes. In only twenty years, they've gone from featuring mind-expanding hashish to fat-reducing prune puree.

This recipe is courtesy of the California Prune Board.

4 ounces unsweetened chocolate
½ cup prune puree (see Note) or
    prepared prune butter
3 large egg whites
1 cup sugar

1 teaspoon salt
1 teaspoon vanilla extract
½ cup all-purpose flour
¼ cup chopped walnuts

Preheat the oven to 350° F. Coat an 8-inch square baking pan with vegetable cooking spray.

Cut the chocolate into 1-inch pieces and place in a heatproof bowl. Set over low heat in a small skillet containing ½ inch simmering water. Stir occasionally just until the chocolate is melted. Remove from the heat; set aside.

In a mixing bowl, combine all the remaining ingredients except the flour and walnuts; beat to blend thoroughly. Mix in the flour. Spread the batter in the prepared pan; sprinkle with the walnuts.

Bake about 30 minutes, until springy to the touch about 2 inches around edges. Cool on a rack. Cut into 1½-inch squares. *Makes 3 dozen.*

NOTE: To make prune puree, combine ⅔ cup (4 ounces) pitted prunes and 3 tablespoons water in the container of a food processor. Pulse on and off until the prunes are finely chopped. *Makes ½ cup.*

CHOCOLATE PINTO BEANS

Not to be shown up by a bunch of prune faces, the USA Dry Pea and Lentil Council has come up with many dessert recipes incorporating dried peas or beans.

Unfortunately this fudge's usefulness as a guessing game is limited by the bean skins' tendency to stick to one's teeth.

1 16-ounce bag semisweet chocolate baking chips	2 tablespoons corn syrup
¾ cup cooked pinto beans, mashed	2 tablespoons sugar
½ cup heavy cream	2 teaspoons vanilla extract
1 14-ounce can sweetened condensed milk	1½ cups chopped walnuts
	½ cup sunflower seeds
	2 cups mini marshmallows

Microwave the chocolate chips, pinto beans, heavy cream, and milk in a large microwave-safe bowl on high 2 to 3 minutes, or until the chocolate is almost melted, stirring halfway through the heating time. Remove from the microwave.

Stir until the chocolate is completely melted. Add corn syrup and sugar and mix with an electric mixer. Stir in the vanilla, walnuts, sunflower seeds, and marshmallows. Spread into a greased 8-inch square pan and refrigerate until firm. Cut into squares. *Makes 2½ pounds.*

MOCK COCONUT PIE

We are saving most of our mock recipes for the chapter on holidays and other special occasions, since eating mock foods is the perfect way to celebrate April Fool's Day. But they also belong in a chapter about surprise ingredients. If they're really good mock recipes, the people who eat them may not realize they contain a surprise but the people who make them will.

This recipe for mock coconut qualifies as really good. In it, grated potatoes supply the texture and moistness of shredded coconut—a hard-to-find ingredient in the 1910s when this recipe was popular.

1 9-inch pie shell	*3 eggs*
3 potatoes	*1 teaspoon grated nutmeg*
2 cups milk	*½ cup sugar*

Make and cook the pie shell per package directions. Preheat the oven to 350°F.

Peel and grate the potatoes, then put them in a sieve and wash them under cold water. Pat the potatoes dry with a paper towel. Put the milk, eggs, nutmeg, and sugar in a medium saucepan and cook over low heat until the mixture thickens slightly. Add the potatoes and stir.

Pour into the pie shell. Bake 30 minutes, or until lightly browned and a knife inserted in the center comes out clean. *Makes 1 9-inch pie.*

MOCK LOBSTER SALAD

Seen the price of lobster lately? If so, you'll have no trouble guessing why mock lobster recipes abound. Many contain haddock and shrimp—and so seem a small accomplishment compared to this Mock Lobster Salad recipe from the Foot Washins chapter of Ernest Matthew Mickler's *Sinkin Spells, Hot Flashes, Fits and Cravins* which contains no fish at all.

¼ pound crackers
1 sweet green pepper, diced
1 cup diced celery

2 hard-boiled eggs, chopped
2 cups tomato juice
1 cup mayonnaise

Crumble the crackers (crackers should be in rather large pieces), add the remaining ingredients, and mix. Tastes like lobster but there's none in it. *2 servings as a main dish; 4 as a side salad.*

SPUD FUDGE

Popular terms such as couch potato and mouse potato lend the potato an unhealthful image which, in this pairing with sugar and fatty peanut butter fat, it richly deserves. Oh, but what an easy and delicious way to turn this healthful vegetable into junk food!

1 medium potato
1 to 2 pounds confectioners' sugar

Peanut butter

Boil, peel, and mash the potato. Add the sugar until all the moisture is absorbed and roll into a ball. Put a thin layer of sugar on a board or piece of wax paper. Roll the potato ball out into a rectangular shape and pie crust thickness.

Cover with a thin layer of peanut butter and then roll up like a jelly roll. Refrigerate for 30 minutes, cut into thin slices, and eat. *Makes about 20 pieces.*

2

ETHNIC ODDITIES

Familiarity may breed contempt, but unfamiliarity does it even better. This is never more true than when it comes to regional, ethnic, or international foods. Any American could argue, for instance, that a recipe for a Fluffernutter sandwich is not strange or unusual enough to be in this book. But only a Japanese-American or maybe a gourmet yuppie could make the same argument about sushi, the Japanese dish commonly featuring seaweed and raw fish.

That's what this chapter consists of: a sampling (and only a sampling) of recipes that—though well known and standard in their own place and time—will seem unusual to the contemporary, average, mainstream American. In other words, in this chapter, we focus on unusual recipes strongly identified with a specific culture rather than any old recipes with unusual ingredients.

Since the average American is by and large a mythical creature, it is likely that you, dear reader of specific ethnic and geographic origins, will find herein recipes that do not seem strange, recipes that you in fact grew up on.

If so, please do not write to tell me. Save your energy for doing something really useful and important, like conning your college professor into letting you cook a bunch of weird Pennsylvania Dutch dishes instead of writing a paper about the people who invented them. This is the "educational" chapter, after all.

PRUNE ICE CREAM

If you thought Baskin-Robbins or Boston's Steve was the originator of unusual ice cream flavors, think again. Prune Ice Cream has been a specialty of the Griswold Inn in Essex, Connecticut, since (constipated?) Yankee colonists dreamed it up.
Its musty flavor begs the question: Could it be the same batch?

6 tablespoons sugar   ½ gallon premium vanilla ice cream
8 to 10 ounces pitted prunes

Dissolve the sugar in 1½ cups water. Add the prunes and soak for 2 days. Drain the prunes and puree well in a food processor. Soften the ice cream. Place in a mixer with the paddle attachment. Add the pureed prunes. Beat at medium speed a few seconds until the prunes are thoroughly incorporated. Refreeze immediately. *Makes 2 quarts.*

CHICKEN WITH CHOCOLATE AND CHILIES (CHICKEN MOLE)

The dark gravy concoction called mole, whose name literally means "concoction", is so standard in Mexico that south-of-the-border supermarkets sell it in the form of an instant paste concentrate. Making mole from scratch there is as unusual as making your own Jell-O would be here.

Unfortunately Campbell's doesn't make condensed mole sauce so you'll have to act like a really serious Mexican cook in order to taste this. (To help you decide whether the work is worth it, this dish is more spicy than sweet, with the chocolate mainly adding richness.)

2 2½-pound chickens, cut in pieces
6 black peppercorns
6 dried chilies
½ cup blanched almonds
1 slice of stale bread, toasted
¼ cup raisins
1 teaspoon ground allspice or
   cinnamon
¼ teaspoon anise seed

1½ tablespoons unsweetened cocoa
3 tablespoons olive oil
1 onion, minced
1 garlic clove
2 tablespoons flour
3 cups tomato sauce
3 cups chicken stock
1 tablespoon sesame seeds, toasted

Put the chicken in a pot with the peppercorns, cover with water, and bring to a boil. Lower heat, cover and simmer until tender, about 2 hours. Let cool, at which time you should pick the meat from the bones. Strain stock.

Tear the chilies into pieces, discard the seeds, and place in a cup of boiling water for 10 minutes. Then put the chilies into a blender along with the almonds, bread, raisins, allspice or cinnamon, anise, and cocoa and blend well.

In a large pot on top of the stove, place the olive oil along with the onion and garlic and cook until the onion is transparent or about 3 minutes. Then add the flour and the contents of the blender. Cook until well mixed and smooth, then add the tomato sauce.

After 5 minutes, add 3 cups of stock from the cooked chicken and bring to a simmer. Place the pieces of chicken into the sauce and then simmer, covered, for 15 minutes, or until the chicken is hot and has assumed the rich brown color of the sauce.

Serve with cooked rice and sprinkled with toasted sesame seeds. *6 to 8 servings.*

CHERRY SOUP

Cold soups containing vegetables are weird enough; then there are ones like this with fruit.

Like gazpacho and cold borscht (beet soup), Cherry Soup is best served in the summer. In fact, the traditional reason given for serving cold soups in summer is that they make people feel cooler.

But I have a feeling the real reason they're popular then is so that hosts and hostesses can explain all that is unconsumed on people's naturally decreased appetites.

Cherry Soup has its roots in Middle Europe where it was often served as a main course. Michigan's Cherry Marketing Institute recommends serving the following version of theirs with a hearty salad.

½ cup frozen unsweetened tart cherries
½ cup frozen dark sweet cherries
1 cup custard-style cherry yogurt
1 cup sour cream

1 cup heavy cream
½ cup dried tart cherries
1 tablespoon grenadine
1 tablespoon sugar, or to taste
¼ teaspoon grated nutmeg

Thaw the tart and sweet cherries, reserving their juice. In an electric blender or food processor container, puree the tart and sweet cherries with juice until smooth. Set aside.

In a large mixing bowl, combine the yogurt, sour cream, heavy cream, and dried cherries; mix well. Add the pureed cherries, grenadine, sugar, and nutmeg; mix well. Let chill 1 to 2 hours to blend the flavors. Serve chilled. *6 servings.*

CRACKER PUDDING

In the days before frozen yogurt and SnackWell's cookies, Americans ate puddings for dessert. Turn-of-the-century skinflints often made them from main-course leftovers such as rice, tapioca, and stale bread.

Crackers were another un-dessert-y ingredient to get the pudding treatment, although this fact is being quickly lost to history. Even those few modern cafeterias, lunch counters, and diners that still serve bread and rice pudding rarely offer the cracker kind.

But now you can.

1 tablespoon salted butter
2 cups crumbled plain soda
   crackers or saltines
1 cup raisins
2½ cups milk

2 eggs, beaten
¾ cup sugar
½ teaspoon cinnamon
½ teaspoon salt

Butter a 3-quart casserole dish. Put the cracker crumbs and raisins into the baking dish. Mix the milk, eggs, sugar, cinnamon, and salt in a bowl and then pour over the crumbs and raisins. Put in the refrigerator and let stand for at least 2 hours.

Preheat the oven to 425° F and bake the pudding for 20 minutes, or until the crackers are brown. *4 to 6 servings.*

FRENCH CREAM PIZZA

Pizza may have been invented by Italians in America but it has been embraced by cultures around the globe. In fact, the well-traveled Domino's Pizza company reports delivering squid-topped pizza to the Japanese, tuna- and corn-adorned ones to the English, and egg-decorated ones to Australians.

But for weird toppings, few can beat the French flambee, a pizza featuring onions, the baconlike lardon, and crème fraîche, or white cream sauce. This is my American interpretation of Domino's French pizza treat.

1 14- to 16-inch uncooked pizza crust
1 cup whipping cream
1 teaspoon cultured buttermilk
2 cups (8 ounces) grated mozzarella
   cheese

4 strips of bacon, cooked and crumbled
   into small pieces
¾ cup chopped onion

Preheat the oven to 450° F.

Mix the whipping cream and buttermilk in a saucepan. Heat to about 85° F, then lower the heat slightly and let stand until thickened. Place the pizza crust on a baking sheet.

Stir the cream mixture, then pour onto the center of the pizza crust and spread evenly (the sauce will not be as thick as tomato pizza sauce). Sprinkle on the cheese, then the bacon and onions.

Place the pizza crust on the bottom rack of the oven and bake until the cheese bubbles, about 10 minutes. Serve immediately with lots of napkins.

STEAK AND KIDNEY PIE

Say all you want about British cooking: Britain is still one of the few cultures to have figured out how to make kidneys into a popular pub food.

I refer of course to steak and kidney pie, a clever case of disguise and distraction caused by mixing this disgusting organ meat with good steak, seasoning it with Worcestershire sauce and wine, and enclosing it all under a delicious, flaky pie crust.

¾ pound kidneys	1 cup red wine
3 tablespoons salted butter	1 teaspoon Worcestershire sauce
1 onion, chopped	Salt and pepper to taste
1 pound chuck or round steak, cut in ¾-inch cubes	¾ cup sliced mushrooms
	3 tablespoons flour
2 cups beef stock	1 uncooked pastry crust

Remove the membrane from the kidneys; cut the kidneys into halves lengthwise, then cut into half-inch cubes. In a large skillet or pot, melt the butter and sauté the onions until translucent. Add the steak and brown. Add the beef stock, wine, Worcestershire sauce, and salt and pepper and simmer, covered, for 1 hour, or until the meat is tender.

Add the kidneys and mushrooms. Thicken the broth by gradually adding flour to the pan, then raising the heat and allowing the sauce to boil for 1 minute. Let cool while you prepare the pastry crust.

Preheat the oven to 425° F.

Pour the cooled meat mixture into a 1½- or 2-quart greased casserole dish. Cover with the pastry and prick the top. Bake for 1 hour, or until the crust is golden. *6 servings.*

CORNCOB JELLY

Even the most thorough corn-on-the-cob eater seems wasteful compared to the midwestern farm types who make this jelly from the bare cobs. It tastes a lot like sugar or honey, which is not surprising, given the ingredients (or lack thereof).

12 bare corncobs
1 1.75-ounce box powdered pectin

4 cups sugar

Boil the corncobs in 4 cups water for at least 10 minutes. Then strain the water and measure out 3 cups. (Water may be added if necessary.) Add the pectin, then bring to a boil. Add the sugar and bring to another boil. Skim, then seal in hot sterilized jars. *Makes 2 pints.*

FRIED CHITLINS

Northerners who eat pork intestine–encased sausages with regularity usually squirm when you suggest they eat chitlins (sometimes spelled chitterlings), even though they are essentially the sausage casing without the stuffing. Ah, but chitlins are a SOUTHERN soul food delicacy and in food as in just about every other area of life, it all depends on what you're used to.

(Brave Northerners who want to try this will have the best luck finding chitlins at butcher shops located in the center of the nearest large city.)

5 pounds fresh chitlins
2 tablespoons whole cloves
1 red chili pepper, cut

2 eggs, beaten
Cornmeal or cracker meal

Cut intestines into 6-inch to 1-foot pieces, then run water through their openings until it runs clear. (Skip this step if purchased precooked.) Remove any excess fat, then slit lengthwise and clean. Put the intestines in salted water and put in the refrigerator for at least an hour.

Add the cloves and chili pepper to the pan of chitlins and water and cook on top of the stove, covered, for 2 to 4 hours, or until tender. Dry the chitlins, then cut into 2-inch squares.

Dip the chitlins in the beaten eggs, then roll them in cornmeal or cracker meal and pan- or deep-fry until brown. *4 to 5 servings.*

SQUID SALAD

Food writer Irena Chalmers describes squid as a "pale white two-eyed torpedo with a bad hairdresser." Few Americans would find her words unfair. But Mediterranean peoples have been eating this inexpensive, quick-to-prepare, slightly chewy fish for at least 1,000 years.

Most Italian-American restaurant menus call squid calamari (the harder for the squeamish to know what it is?) and serve it cut up and fried or in a salad like this.

1½ pounds squid, cut into
    ¼-inch rounds
⅓ cup olive oil
⅓ cup white wine vinegar
½ teaspoon oregano

⅛ teaspoon dried red pepper flakes
1 cup stuffed green olives, quartered
1 cup chopped celery
Lemon wedges

Rinse the squid under cold water. Cut off the tentacles and the head and remove the body filling, including the transparent quill-like backbone. Slice what you have left into ¼-inch rings.

Whisk the olive oil, vinegar, oregano, and pepper flakes together in a bowl. Add the olives and celery and mix.

Blanch the squid pieces in salted boiling water until the circles curl, no more than a minute or they will get tough. Drain and then immediately mix into the bowl with the other ingredients.

Cover and refrigerate for at least 30 minutes before serving with lemon wedges. *6 servings.*

PEANUT SOUP

Like the roots of some of America's best original music, peanut butter soup came to America with the African slaves. Its rich thick texture makes it perfect to serve on a cold winter's night.

Because it contains one of kids' favorite foods, it's one of a few "weird" foods they will willingly eat. (Most of the other weird foods kids will eat look like bodily secretions and can be found in Chapters 6 and 8.)

Adults who can't conceive of sipping peanut butter may just need to be reminded that peanuts are beans—and that this soup is therefore really no weirder than split pea or minestrone. This recipe was supplied by the Peanut Advisory Board.

2 tablespoons (¼ stick) salted butter
2 tablespoons grated onion
1 celery stalk, thinly sliced
2 tablespoons flour
3 cups chicken broth

½ cup creamy peanut butter
¼ teaspoon salt
1 cup light cream
2 tablespoons roasted peanuts, chopped
½ cup hot pepper jelly (optional)

Melt the butter in a saucepan over low heat; add the onion and celery. Sauté for about 5 minutes. Add the flour and mix until well blended. Stir in the chicken broth and allow it to simmer for about 30 minutes. Remove from the heat; strain the broth.

Stir the peanut butter, salt, and cream into the strained broth until well mixed. Serve hot. Garnish each serving with a teaspoon of chopped peanuts and a dollop of jelly, if desired. *4 servings.*

WATER TOAST

It's hard to believe this could be anything but the accidental result of putting a loaf of bread too close to the sink. But no, it is an actual recipe that appears in several sources from the turn of the century and early 1900s.

Judging from those books, Water Toast seems to have been a low-cal variation on milk toast, a popular lunch counter and hotel breakfast dish of the era that consisted of toast soaked in milk and coated with butter and sugar.

If milk toast was primarily eaten by old people (as its derogatory nicknames "graveyard stew" and "toothless gruel," might lead one to believe), then water toast would seem best suited to the old and fat.

Salt
4 slices thick white bread, well
  toasted

Butter
2 tomato slices (optional)
Iceberg lettuce (optional)

Boil some salted water, then dip the toast into it. Spread with butter and eat immediately with or without tomato and lettuce garnish. *2 servings.*

SHREDDED WHEAT BISCUIT CHOCOLATE JELLY

You'll find most brand name food excesses in chapter 3, Fashions and Obsessions. This shredded wheat recipe is here because it dates back to the product's turn-of-the-century creation by Henry D. Perky.

Perky originally marketed shredded wheat as a cure for indigestion that was adaptable to almost any meal or recipe. To drive the point home he opened a Denver restaurant with an all–shredded wheat menu. It included shredded wheat mashed potatoes, cakes, ice cream, coffee, and this weirdest of creations, shredded wheat crumb-filled chocolate gelatin.

(Warning: Some of the commercial products called for in the original recipe no longer exist, so we can't guarantee this is the dish Mr. Perky made.)

1 envelope unflavored gelatin	½ cup sugar
1 pint milk	Pinch of salt
⅔ cup shredded wheat biscuit crumbs	1 egg
1 1-ounce square unsweetened baking chocolate	½ teaspoon vanilla extract
	¼ cup heavy or whipping cream, whipped

Blend the gelatin with ⅓ cup cold water, then ½ cup boiling water and mix well. Put the milk, shredded wheat biscuit crumbs, and chocolate in a pan on the stovetop and heat until the milk scalds, then for 10 minutes beyond that.

In a separate bowl, beat the sugar, salt, and egg together, then add to the ingredients in the saucepan and cook for 3 minutes. Remove the pan from the stove. Then stir in the gelatin and vanilla, and finally, the whipped cream.

Pour the whole thing into a cold gelatin mold and put into the refrigerator for 2 hours or until hardened. *6 servings.*

LAZY MODERN VERSION: Melt semisweet chocolate chips in a bowl in the microwave. Dip shredded wheat in it and eat.

BRUNSWICK STEW

Brunswick Stew is a classic southern small game dish variously credited to African slaves and to a Brunswick County, Virginia, politician. A true Brunswick must contain either squirrel or rabbit and okra, lima beans, corn, rice, and tomatoes.

Alas, wimpy moderns usually substitute chicken for the game. Before YOU do you should know about a study conducted by Los Angeles's Institute for Sexual Longevity where subjects reported better sex lives with regular consumption of Bugs Bunny's kin.

Salt and pepper
2 to 2½ pounds squirrel or rabbit
   meat, cut up
2 onions, sliced
1 tablespoon butter
1 teaspoon chopped fresh parsley
1 bay leaf

1 16-ounce can whole or stewed
   tomatoes
2 teaspoons Worcestershire sauce
1 cup rice
1 8½-ounce can lima beans
1 cup sliced okra (fresh or canned)
1 15¼-ounce can corn

Salt and pepper the squirrel or rabbit pieces. In a large skillet, brown the onions in butter and then add the meat and brown on all sides.

Put the onions and meat in a large stockpot and add the parsley, bay leaf, 2 cups water, tomatoes, and Worcestershire sauce. Cook until bubbling, then simmer, covered, at least an hour, or until the hind leg of the squirrel or rabbit can be pierced with a fork.

Add the rice and cook for 5 to 7 minutes. Add the lima beans, okra, and corn and simmer an additional 30 minutes.

The stew should be thick enough to eat with a fork (the thickness can be adjusted by adding water or bread crumbs). *5 to 7 servings.*

OATMEAL SOUP

Quaker Oats Instant Oatmeal is now sold in S'mores, Cookies 'n Cream, and Fruity Marshmallow flavors. But as far as we know not even Quaker has ever tried to take hot oatmeal into other parts of the day via the addition of vegetables.

This just goes to prove how desperate things were in England during World War II, when and where this recipe was created.

2 tablespoons (¼ stick) margarine or salted butter	Salt and pepper
2 onions, finely diced	1 cup milk
2 tablespoons oatmeal	3 carrots, grated

Melt the margarine in a stockpot on top of the stove, add the onions, and sauté for 5 minutes, or until translucent.

Mix the oatmeal with a pint of cold water, then put into the pot with the onions and bring to a boil. Season with salt and pepper. Simmer for 30 minutes, stirring frequently.

Add the milk and carrots and simmer an additional 15 minutes. *4 servings.*

SCRAPPLE

Pennsylvanians have been scaring visitors with this porridge and pork dish since the early 1800s. Scrapple is usually sliced and fried and served alongside eggs for breakfast or brunch, and is cookin' cousins to the equally reviled haggis, a pork-and-oatmeal–stuffed sausage from Scotland.

Scrapple is traditionally made from pork scraps or a hog's head. Some modern cookbooks prettify the dish by calling for sausage or regular pieces of boned pork. But if you're reading this book, we assume you're made of stronger stuff.

3 to 4 pounds pork scraps
   (with bones) or 1 hog's head,
   split
1 teaspoon sage
1 teaspoon salt

½ teaspoon pepper
2 cups cornmeal (or about 1⅛ times
   the amount of minced meat
   obtained)
Bacon fat

Put the pork scraps or hog's head into a pot of water, bring to a boil, and simmer, covered, for 2 to 3 hours, or until the meat falls off the bones. Remove the meat, slice, and mince it. Strain and degrease the cooking water.

Put the minced meat into a clean pot along with twice its volume of the degreased cooking water. Add the sage, salt, and pepper and bring to a boil. Gradually add the cornmeal, stirring until well thickened, about 30 minutes.

Pour into a 9 x 5-inch loaf pan and chill until firm, about 4 hours. Unmold, cut into ½-inch slices, and brown in bacon fat. *6 to 8 servings.*

VINEGAR PIE

Dessert pies traditionally feature one or another fruit- or milk-filled puddings or custards. Then there is that small subgroup of pies that bear silent witness to the fact that most people view pies as an excuse to enjoy sugar and fat—and so to hell with the healthful milk or fruit!

They include the southern chess pie, Pennsylvania Dutch shoofly, the midwestern sugar and this 100-year-old way of enjoying pie with something you'll find in the cupboard at almost any time of year.

2 unbaked, 8-inch piecrusts
1 teaspoon flour
1 teaspoon sugar

1 tablespoon vinegar
½ teaspoon grated nutmeg
1 egg, beaten

Preheat the oven to 375° F.

Line a pie pan with half the dough. Blend 1 cup water with the remaining ingredients in a bowl, then pour into the dough-lined pan. Cover pie with the rest of the dough, prick the dough in several places with a fork, and bake about 40 minutes, or until the crust is brown and a knife inserted between the center and the edge of the pie comes out clean. *Makes 1 8-inch pie.*

BIRD'S NEST SOUP

A soup fashioned from an ordinary bird's nest made of twigs and dried leaves would be strange enough. But this soup is made from the nest of a particular type of cave-dwelling Asian swallow which spins its nest out of ITS OWN DRIED SALIVA!

Despite this, the Chinese consider bird's nests to be a delicacy on the order of shark's fins. Actually, fishing for shark is fun compared to scrambling around the odoriferous guano-encrusted cave floors and slippery ledges and crevasses where the nests are found.

1 6-ounce box of bird's nest (see
    Ingredients Sources)
6 to 8 cups chicken broth
2 to 4 dried Chinese mushrooms,
    soaked and sliced
4 water chestnuts, coarsely chopped

1 to 2 pounds bite-size pieces cooked
    chicken meat
3 ounces cooked ham, chopped
½ tablespoon cornstarch, mixed with
    several drops of water to form a
    paste
½ teaspoon salt

Cover the bird's nest with water and soak for 1 hour. Pick out foreign substances, if any. Set aside.

Add the chicken broth, mushrooms, chestnuts, cooked chicken, and ham to the pot and cook for 10 minutes. Add the cornstarch mixture and salt and cook, stirring, another 5 minutes or until hot. Drain the bird's nest, then divide it into 6 to 8 sections and arrange at the bottom of shallow soup bowls in the shape of bird's nests.

Ladle the soup into the center of each bowl. *6 to 8 servings.*

STEAK TARTARE

Steak Tartare is a dish of seasoned chopped raw lean beef invented by the medieval Tartars and taken up by the French. Suffice it to say, this was long before anyone had ever heard of Jack In The Box hamburgers, *E. coli,* or salmonella.

Between the food poisoning potential and the idea of eating raw meat, this dish is now less a repast than a test of courage, mettle, and (some would say) foolhardiness.

*12 ounces tenderloin or top sirloin
steak
Dash of salt and pepper
1 tablespoon vegetable oil
2 teaspoons Dijon mustard*

*Dash of hot pepper sauce
1 onion, finely minced
2 tablespoons chopped capers
1 teaspoon chopped fresh parsley
2 egg yolks*

Coarsely grind the steak in a grinder or finely chop it with a knife. Place in a bowl, then mix the meat with salt and pepper, oil, mustard, and pepper sauce.

Divide the meat in half and place on serving plates, making a small indentation in the center of each. In a clean bowl, mix the onion, capers, and parsley.

Place 1 egg yolk in the center of each meat indentation, then garnish with the onion, capers, and parsley mixture. *2 servings.*

SUGAR ON SNOW

Maple syrup and snow are two things the state of Vermont produces in great quantity. The way this organic Sno-Kone-in-a-bowl combines the two is simplicity itself, which should make it attractive to sugarholics and cooking illiterates beyond the state's borders.

Several handfuls of clean, newly fallen snow

⅓ to ½ cup pure Vermont maple syrup

Harvest the snow and place it in a soup bowl. Pour on the maple syrup. Eat with a spoon. *1 serving.*

STEWED PRETZELS

This is more or less the Pennsylvania version of Sugar on Snow: that is to say, a very simple dish served in a bowl featuring a local specialty enjoyed and understood mainly by locals—which itself seems curious, considering how many Americans eat dough in milk for breakfast.

1 pint milk
2 tablespoons (¼ stick) salted butter
1 large soft pretzel (if you can't buy these locally, use a supermarket frozen brand such as SuperPretzel)

Pork breakfast sausage (optional)

Warm the milk, divide equally between 2 soup bowls, and dot each with 1 tablespoon butter. Break the pretzel into pieces and throw them into the milk. If desired, add some pieces of browned sausage. *2 servings.*

BEET PUDDING

This is a Carolina dessert tradition that some say beats all; others, that it simply beats.

3 large eggs, separated
2 tablespoons cornstarch
½ teaspoon salt
¾ cup sugar

2 tablespoons (¼ stick) salted butter, melted
1½ cups milk or half-and-half, heated
2¼ cups shredded beets

Preheat the oven to 350° F.

Beat the egg yolks, then stir in the cornstarch, salt, sugar, melted butter, and hot milk. Whip the egg whites until soft peaks form, then fold into the mixture with the beets.

Pour into a 9 x 9-inch casserole dish and bake for 45 to 55 minutes, or until a knife inserted in the center comes out clean. *6 to 8 servings.*

SUSHI

Most people associate sushi with raw fish. The word actually refers to the vinegar-seasoned rice that is served with the raw fish and, if that isn't disgusting enough, wrapped with seaweed.

Some Japanese chefs study for ten years to learn how to cut, wrap, and present sushi properly. So the result of the highly simplified instructions you're going to get here could very well leave a more exaggerated sense of sushi's strangeness than it deserves.

1 cup short-grain white rice
1/3 pound tuna or other fresh raw fish
1/4 cup unseasoned rice vinegar
1 tablespoon sugar
1/2 teaspoon salt

3 sheets nori seaweed, 7½ by 4 inches
or cut to that size (sold in most
Asian markets and health food
stores)
Wasabi (also sold in Asian markets) or
horseradish paste (optional)

Cook the rice according to package directions. While the rice cooks, put the fish on a cutting board and slice into ¼-inch-thick strips the length of your nori rectangle. (Cut straight down so you do not tear the fish.)

Put the vinegar, sugar, and salt in a small saucepan and heat until the sugar dissolves. Toast the nori pieces by passing them over a gas flame one side at a time for a few seconds, or until crisp.

Pour the cooked rice into a cool pan or dish and mix with the seasoned mixture. Put the pan into the refrigerator for a few minutes and then stir some more.

Place the nori shiny side down on a clean, damp kitchen cloth with the 7½-inch side facing you and spread about ⅔ cup rice in a layer to cover it to within about a quarter inch of the edges.

Run some wasabi along the edge of the tuna strip, if desired. Then place the tuna in the center of the rectangle and begin rolling the seaweed over the rice, leaving the cloth behind as you go. (Wet your hands with vinegar and water periodically and the rice will be easier to handle.) Cut each roll into 6 pieces and serve. *3 to 4 servings.*

GOOD NEWS FOR THE SQUEAMISH: Some fish used in sushi are precooked. The bad news: They include octopus and eel.

POLLEN PANCAKES

This recipe for cattail Pollen Pancakes is here instead of in Chapter 4, Flora and Fauna, because they were long-ago favorites of Native American Indians—obviously not a people who had problems with allergies.

1 cup cattail pollen (see Note)
1 cup white or wheat flour
3 teaspoons baking powder
2 large eggs, slightly beaten

1½ cups milk
2 tablespoons (¼ stick) salted butter,
* melted*

Mix the dry and wet ingredients separately, then together. Cook in a lightly greased frying pan as you would any pancakes, turning after small bubbles form and the edges of the pancakes become dry, about 3 minutes. *Makes about 16 large pancakes.*

NOTE: To harvest cattail pollen: When the cattail head is still a thin green stalk (usually in May or June), bend the stalk and shake the head over a bowl so that it catches the golden pollen. Put the pollen through a sieve to remove any debris.

PEPPER POT SOUP

There is a curious kind of symmetry to eating tripe (animal stomach). It's sort of like those drawings that show someone standing next to a television that contains an image of them standing next to a television that shows a picture. . . . You get the idea.

Many of the best-known recipes featuring tripe seem to use it in soup. The Italians have their busecca; the Mexicans, their menudo; and we Americans, our Pepper Pot Soup.

In fact, Pepper Pot Soup has an important place in American history as one of the things that kept George Washington's starving army alive at Valley Forge, thus saving Americans from a fate of warm beer and steak and kidney pie.

½ pound parboiled honeycomb tripe, cooked and diced (honeycomb is the most tender kind—which, considering how tough this stuff is, is like saying someone is "the nicest death row inmate")
2 tablespoons (¼ stick) salted butter
1 onion, minced
1 celery stalk, chopped
1 green pepper, chopped
1 large potato, peeled and diced
5 cups veal or chicken broth or stock
½ teaspoon freshly ground pepper
2 tablespoons flour
½ cup heavy cream

If not already purchased precooked, wash and cook the tripe in a big pot of boiling water until tender, at least 6 hours. If it has already been cooked, you'll only have to parboil it in salted water for 15 minutes. Dice into small pieces.

Melt the butter in a large pot, add all the vegetables except the potato, and sauté for 15 minutes. Add the potato, and cook another 5 minutes. Add the stock, tripe, and pepper, then bring to a boil.

Simmer, partially covered, about 20 minutes or until the potato and tripe are tender. Add about 1 tablespoon water to the flour to make a paste, then add to the soup. Just before serving, add the cream and reheat slowly. *4 servings.*

RED BEANS AND SWEET CORN FROZEN DELIGHT

The first and only time I ever had this dessert was at a wonderful restaurant in suburban New Haven, Connecticut, called Bentara. Chef Hasni Ghazali calls it "ABC" and says it is unique to his native Malaysia, although I have seen some Taiwanese and Philippine puddings that contain milk, sugar, and beans or corn.

Notice I said "seen," not tasted. Now that I know my ABC I am too smart to want to learn about any other unusual Asian desserts.

½ cup plus 3 tablespoons sugar
⅛-inch slice peeled ginger
1 whole clove
1 teaspoon red food coloring
1 15-ounce can cooked red beans
1 8-ounce can creamed corn

1 20-ounce can palm seed in syrup
  (sold in Asian groceries)
4 tablespoons grass jelly (sold in Asian
  groceries) or Jell-O (any flavor)
2 pounds shaved or crushed ice
1 12-ounce can evaporated milk

Put ½ cup sugar into a saucepan with ¼ cup water. Add the slice of ginger and the clove. Cook over low heat for several minutes, then add the red food coloring. Set aside.

Empty the can of beans into a saucepan. Turn the heat to low, then add 3 tablespoons sugar and ¼ cup water and cook until almost all the water evaporates.

Divide the bean mixture equally among 4 deep dessert dishes, followed by layers of creamed corn, palm seed, and grass jelly or prepared gelatin. Add a layer of shaved ice. Pour the red syrup and evaporated milk on top. The dishes should resemble red mountains covered with white snow. Serve immediately. *4 servings.*

CASTOR OIL COOKIES

Today's medicine for children tastes so good druggists put on locking caps to keep kids away. But there was no danger of anyone overdosing on the awful-tasting turn-of-the-century cure-all castor oil. That's probably why some smart turn-of-the-century moms slipped it into spice cookies.

½ cup dark brown sugar
¼ cup molasses
¼ cup castor oil
½ teaspoon salt
½ teaspoon baking soda
¼ teaspoon baking powder

¼ teaspoon ginger
¼ teaspoon ground cloves
¼ teaspoon cinnamon
¼ teaspoon grated nutmeg
½ cup milk
Approximately 1 cup flour

Preheat the oven to 400° F.

Mix everything but the flour together in a bowl. Add the flour, a little at a time, until the dough is of rolling consistency. Put the dough in the refrigerator for several hours, then roll to a ¼-inch thickness and cut into desired shapes. Bake on greased cookie sheets for 6 to 8 minutes. *Makes about 40 cookies.*

3

FASHIONS AND OBSESSIONS

What makes someone decide to fashion a pie crust out of cereal crumbs or ice cream out of avocados? It's usually money, supplied by a food trade association that is sponsoring a contest, a food company with a kitchen full of home economists, or a publisher or restaurant owner with eyes on exploiting the popularity of a certain food.

But along with the money there is also often love. Nobody is paying me to put chocolate chips in as many things as I do, for instance. Admittedly, it's harder to believe that love was the motivation for the many recipes that exist for okra and anchovies.

In these cases the love may have more to do with the drive to create new food combinations. In other words, the spirit of experimentation that gave us the Salk vaccine is now alive and well in the people who fill America's church cookbooks with new Jell-O salad combinations. If this isn't a reason to God bless America, I don't know what is.

But whatever the motivation, whatever the situation that created the following recipes, the impression they leave is of chefs obsessed; people who have gotten carried away with their passion for bananas, doughnuts, or whatever it might be. And doesn't just about everything worthwhile in this world come from someone who was at least little bit overinvolved or crazy?

WHITE CASTLE LASAGNE

White Castle was the nation's first fast-food hamburger chain, and some believe there has been little progress in the field since. Is that because of the way the meat and onions are steamed on those tiny buns? The fact that most stores are open twenty-four hours a day? The limited market area that turns every transplanted midwestern and southeastern fan into a slider-starved fanatic?

It's hard to say, but in 1987 the company tried to answer the nationwide demand for their so-called belly-bombers with frozen White Castles boxed and sold in the supermarket. That effectively opened up the company's annual recipe contest to Castlemaniacs across the country.

All recipe entries must contain at least ten White Castle hamburgers or cheeseburgers. The Grand prize is a sack of ten White Castle hamburgers every week for a full year.

Here's a winning dish from the company's 1994 contest that uses the various parts of the burgers as separate ingredients.

1 8-ounce package wide noodles
1 4-ounce can mushrooms
1 14-ounce jar prepared spaghetti
   sauce

10 fresh or frozen White Castle
   hamburgers
1 cup mozzarella cheese, shredded
Garlic salt
Soft butter, salted

Heat the oven to 350° F.

Cook all of the noodles in boiling water for about 10 minutes, or until done. Drain. Place half of the noodles in a buttered 1-quart loaf pan.

Drain the mushrooms and add to the spaghetti sauce. Pour 1 cup of the mushroom-spaghetti sauce over the noodles. If using frozen White Castles, cook them according to package directions. Remove the White Castle hamburgers from their buns and place 5 of the patties on top of the sauce.

Sprinkle ½ cup of shredded mozzarella on top. Add the remaining noodles and repeat the process. Bake until the cheese melts and begins to brown, about 12 minutes.

Place the remaining buns in a glass dish. Brush heavily with garlic butter made by combining the garlic salt with soft butter and place under the broiler for a minute or two for a garlic bread accompaniment. *4 to 6 servings.*

AVOCADO ICE CREAM

America's ice cream palette has broadened considerably since the days when the classic vanilla-chocolate-strawberry carton was an innovation. Thanks to Baskin-Robbins, Steve's, Ben & Jerry's, and upscale independent shops across the country, ice creams filled with cereal, candy, and cookies have become so ordinary they're in every corner grocery.

Fortunately weirdness is still in plentiful supply in California, as are the avocados that are the focal point of this ice cream. And like everything else in California, this ice cream is also cool and smooth.

2 tablespoons lemon juice
2 large ripe avocados, peeled, stoned,
  and mashed

2¼ cups heavy cream
¾ cup sugar
½ teaspoon almond extract (optional)

Mix the lemon juice with the mashed avocados in a bowl. Then heat the cream with the sugar in a saucepan, stirring until the sugar dissolves.

Cool the cream mixture, then mix with the avocado and almond extract, if used, and beat together until smooth. Freeze in an ice cream maker according to the manufacturer's directions. *Makes about a quart.*

PANCAKES CANNED CORN

I feel lucky to have been alive in the era when chocolate chips, pecans, bananas, and coconut all first came to be put in pancake batter. Unfortunately the same spirit of experimentation that brought about chocolate chip banana pancakes has also resulted in Pancakes Canned Corn, a dish in the extremely limited cooking repertoire of several dads of my acquaintance.

Before you recoil in horror or turn the page, think for a minute about the main ingredient in the Native American jonnycakes. It too is corn, albeit in a ground and dried-up form.

Like cornbread, Pancakes Canned Corn tastes best served with ham and lots of butter. Fans are divided on the syrup issue.

1 cup commercial pancake mix
¾ cup milk
1 egg

2 teaspoons vegetable oil
1 8-ounce can whole kernel corn,
 drained

Mix together the pancake mix, milk, egg, oil, and drained corn and cook according to package directions. *3 to 4 servings.*

SPUD PIZZA

If you're thirty or older you can probably remember a time when pizza meant a 16-inch-diameter circle of dough covered with tomato sauce, cheese, and perhaps sausage or pepperoni. No more. Now pizza seems to refer only to a flat crusted form of delivery of anything from barbecued chicken, to clams, to bacon and eggs, to ice cream sundaes (the latter on a graham cracker pie crust pressed onto a pizza pan).

Red potato pizza is among the weirder recipes to feature a traditional thrown-dough crust (and it seems to us that anything called pizza should at least have that). This best-selling creation of Willington, Connecticut, Pizza House chef Richard Rogers is also delicious enough to have captured first place in the exotic category of *Pizza Today* magazine's 1994 Pizza Festiva recipe contest.

1 cup sour cream
1 10-inch uncooked pizza crust
1 pound red potatoes, boiled
    until tender and thinly sliced
1/3 pound sharp cheddar cheese,
    sliced

4 slices cooked and crumbled bacon
1 bunch fresh uncooked broccoli
1 tablespoon chopped fresh chives

Heat the oven to 450° F.

Lay crust on a pizza stone, screen or baking sheet. Spread a thin layer of sour cream onto the pizza shell, cover with the boiled, sliced potatoes, then cover with the cheese and bacon, and garnish with the broccoli. Bake on lowest oven rack about 10 minutes or until crispy, and garnish with chopped chives. *2 to 3 servings.*

DATE SHAKE

No, by this name we do not mean to explain a way to escape a particularly miserable romantic pairing, but rather to give a name to a drink from the days when health food was at once unusual, natural, and full of calories. This is based on a recipe supplied by Indio, California's National Date Festival committee.

2 scoops vanilla ice cream   *2 tablespoons finely chopped dates*
¾ cup milk

Put all the ingredients in a blender and mix. *1 serving.*

HOT RICE BREAKFAST CEREAL

I am not among the Americans who consider steamin' hot grains a breakfast. (Warm donuts are more my speed.) Those who do probably will not regard the idea of eating a hot bowl of rice and prunes for breakfast to be as strange and unappealing as I do.

Not surprisingly, the idea and the recipe comes from Riviana, maker of the Mahatma, Carolina, and River brands of rice.

3 cups plain cooked Mahatma,   *1 tablespoon tub margarine*
   Carolina, or River brown rice   *1 teaspoon cinnamon*
2 cups 1% milk   *Honey or light brown sugar (optional)*
½ cup chopped prunes   *Fresh fruit (optional)*

Combine the rice, milk, prunes, margarine, and cinnamon in a 2- to 3-quart saucepan and bring to a boil. Stir. Reduce the heat to medium-low; cover and simmer 8 to 10 minutes, or until thickened.

Serve with honey or brown sugar and fresh fruit, if desired. *6 servings.*

NOTE TO LAZY PERSONS: Nabisco has just recently come out with a Cream of Rice companion to their Cream of Wheat hot cereal that is doubtless even easier to prepare.

HANDCREAM DIP

Giga Bites bills itself as the official guide to computer hacker cuisine, and author Jenz Johnson claims this pudding and mayonnaise chip dip to be a longtime favorite at parties they frequent.

Since I've always made it my business to stay away from gatherings of computer nerds, large and small, I can not vouch for the accuracy of this statement.

But the recipe works and is certainly weird, from its ingredients to its appearance to its appearance-inspired name.

3 cups prepared vanilla pudding
½ cup mayonnaise
1 pound chocolate candy (such as M&M's or Reese's Pieces)

Dash of black pepper (for zest)
Dash of salt
Dash of paprika (for garnish)

Combine all of the ingredients except the paprika in a large bowl and mix well. The pudding and mayonnaise should completely coat and cover the candy.

Shake the paprika on top.

Serve chilled with salty chips or crackers. *2 to 4 servings.*

BLACK-EYED PEA GUACA-JELL-O SALAD

I would not want to be a judge at a weird Jell-O recipe contest. Between Jell-O cakes and frosting, molded salads with cream cheese and Coke, and Jell-O food art, there would be just too great a possibility for a hung jury.

Still, I'll bet this first-place winning salad from Athens, Texas's 1971 Black-Eyed Pea Jamboree would also be a strong Jell-O contest contender. The creator was one highly imaginative Mrs. Ted Thornton.

1 10-ounce package frozen black-eyed peas
3 slices of bacon (for flavoring)
2 teaspoons pepper sauce
1 ³/₁₀-ounce bottle green food coloring
1 9¾-ounce jar Indian relish
2 tablespoons jalapeño relish
1 6-ounce package lime Jell-O

1 20-ounce can black-eyed peas
2 tablespoons salad oil
3 avocados, peeled and mashed with lemon juice
½ cup finely chopped onion
½ cup diced celery
Lettuce and tomatoes

Bring 3 cups salted water to a boil in a saucepan. Add the frozen black-eyed peas, bacon, pepper sauce, and green food coloring and cook gently for 35 minutes. Remove the bacon and set aside. Drain the peas and place them in a bowl to marinate with the Indian and jalapeño relishes.

Bring 2 cups water to a boil in another saucepan. Pour it over the lime Jell-O and stir until dissolved, then add 2 cups cold water. Chill until partially set.

Meanwhile, heat the contents of can of black-eyed peas and salad oil in a saucepan until warm, then drain. Add the mashed avocados, onion, and celery, then the pea and relish mixture. Blend this with the partially set lime Jell-O.

Pour into a mold and chill until firm. Cut and serve on lettuce with cherry tomatoes or tomato slices. *10 to 12 servings.*

CHOCOLATE SOUP

Some foodies say there are no new recipes, just new ideas on how to make or serve the same old ones. Well, I got the idea of serving cocoa as soup from Jane and Michael Stern's delightful *Square Meals.*

It would make the perfect soup course in an all-chocolate dinner that could also include Yoo-Hoo cocktails, chocolate-dipped pretzels or potato chips hors d'oeuvres, followed by a main course of Hershey's cocoa chili (see page 11) or chicken mole (page 26) and your favorite chocolate dessert.

1 cup milk
½ cup heavy cream
2 tablespoons unsweetened cocoa

2 tablespoons sugar
¼ teaspoon vanilla extract
¼ teaspoon cinnamon

Pour all but a couple of tablespoons of the milk and cream into a saucepan and heat without allowing to boil.

Mix the cocoa, sugar, vanilla, and cinnamon together in a soup bowl with the reserved milk and cream. Then pour into the pan with the hot milk and cream mixture and blend well.

Pour back into the soup bowl and serve with animal crackers or mini marshmallows. *1 serving.*

LAZY PERSON'S VERSION: Follow the directions for 2 cups on a hot chocolate mix except substitute milk and/or cream for most if not all the water.

ASTRONAUT PIE

The General Foods test kitchens never have given the orange juice of the astronauts the same attention as Cool Whip and Jell-O. Maybe that's because of how hard it is to cook in a spacecraft. In fact, we probably have Cool Whip to thank that this blending of real and ersatz foods even exists.

1 9-inch graham cracker piecrust
⅓ cup Tang crystals
1 8-ounce cup sour cream

1 14-ounce can sweetened condensed milk
1 8-ounce tub Cool Whip

Preheat the oven to 375° F. Crisp the piecrust in it for 5 minutes.

In a bowl, blend the Tang, sour cream, milk, and half of the Cool Whip. Place in the piecrust, then top with the remaining Cool Whip. Chill and serve. *8 servings.*

BEER SORBET

Here's a way to "tap" into the simultaneous but somewhat contradictory interests in microbrewery beers and low-fat sorbet frozen desserts while at the same time making good use of those half-drunk bottles of beer lying around the house after a party.

While we're on the subject, why DO so many people not finish beer at parties? Is it just one person who goes around taking two sips out of twenty bottles?

One free pint of beer sorbet to anyone who can solve the mystery.

1 12-ounce bottle dark beer, flat and warm

1 7-ounce can Pilsner beer, flat and warm
⅓ cup sugar

Pour the beer into a bowl and add sugar, mixing until the sugar dissolves. Put into an ice cream maker and freeze according to the manufacturer's directions. *Makes about a quart.*

NOTE TO THOSE TOO DRUNK TO FOLLOW MANUFACTURER'S DIRECTIONS: We have heard of at least one northwest microbrew chain that serves beer floats made by simply putting a scoop of vanilla ice cream into some stout. (We have also heard that it doesn't sell real well.)

JERKY CAKE

Some might argue that "jerky" would be a good adjective for any number of recipes in this book. But in the case of this cake, the term is appropriate in more than one way. The recipe comes from Mary Bell, who was driven to create it by *Just Jerky,* her 132-page book devoted entirely to recipes for making and using the dried meat.

8 1-inch by 5-inch flat jerky sticks for ½ cup dried jerky powder	*1 16.75-ounce box 1-step angel food cake mix*

Freeze or refrigerate jerky sticks, then grind into a powder in a food processor. Make the angel food cake according to the instructions on the box. Add the jerky powder after the cake is completely blended and stir only enough to mix thoroughly. Bake according to the package directions. The cake should be cool before frosting. *12 servings.*

To make frosting: Add 2 tablespoons ground jerky to boxed or jarred fluffy white frosting. Decorate the frosted cake with 1 teaspoon shredded jerky (as you would with shredded chocolate or coconut).

HOT DOG PIE

M ost people are perfectly happy to eat hot dogs in buns. Most people are also pretty boring. But no one will say this about you when you serve them this hot dog adaptation of a traditional French-Canadian pork pie. (I can't guarantee they won't say anything else bad about you, though.)

2 medium potatoes, finely chopped
1 onion, finely chopped
6 to 7 hot dogs, finely chopped
½ cup sauerkraut, drained
Bread crumbs

¾ teaspoon mustard powder (or to taste)
¼ teaspoon caraway seeds
2 unbaked 8- or 9-inch piecrusts (top and bottom)
Milk

Put the potatoes, onion, and ½ cup water into a large pot and cook on top of the stove over low to medium heat, stirring occasionally, for about 15 minutes. Add the hot dogs and sauerkraut and continue cooking and stirring another 10 minutes or until potatoes are tender.

Preheat the oven to 350° F.

Drain the excess water if any, from the pan, and add the bread crumbs to thicken. (The mixture should still be somewhat moist.) Gradually mix in the mustard and caraway seeds and adjust the seasoning to taste.

Put the mixture into the bottom piecrust and cover with top piecrust, pricking holes in it with a fork and dressing the top with milk to help it brown. Put it in the oven and bake until the crust is golden, about an hour. *6 to 8 servings.*

CAT KEBABS

Once upon a time people only served their pets table scraps or leftovers. Now there are tons of pet cookbooks and even one Philadelphia restaurant (Cafe Sorella) where dogs and their owners are invited to dine together.

The next step, obviously, is to cook at home for the WHOLE family, not just its human members. This recipe is designed to meet the taste and nutritional needs of households headed by cats.

½ cup soy sauce
¼ cup white wine
2 tablespoons lemon juice
2 tablespoons dark brown sugar
½ teaspoon garlic powder
¾ pound tuna or swordfish steak, cut into 1½-inch chunks

Vegetables and fruits of your choice, cut in skewerable chunks (mushrooms, cherry tomatoes, pearl onions, bell peppers, zucchini, and pineapple, for example)
¼ teaspoon corn oil
Dash of iodized salt
½ teaspoon bone meal (available at pet food stores)

Combine the soy sauce, white wine, lemon juice, brown sugar, and garlic powder in a bowl to make a marinade. Add the fish chunks and coat thoroughly with the marinade. Cover and refrigerate at least 4 hours.

Preheat a charcoal grill or oven broiler and place the fish chunks on skewers along with the vegetables and fruits of your choice.

Grill 6 to 7 minutes per side, basting with marinade occasionally. For people, serve with rice and salad.

To prepare for kitty: Cut the fish and finely chop some vegetables in a bowl with some rice. Add the corn oil, salt and bone meal, mix thoroughly, and serve cool. *Serves 1 person and 2 cats.*

TABASCO ICE CREAM

Spicy desserts are hot right now—both literally and figuratively. Employees of expensive restaurants these days are adding hot pepper or hot sauce to gingerbread, brownies, cookies, and fruitcake with the enthusiasm of culinary pyromaniacs.

Even more disconcerting than desserts that are spicy and sugary are those that are spicy, sugary, and cold as in the following recipe from Tabasco pepper sauce maker McIlhenny Company.

½ cup milk
1 medium cinnamon stick
1 strip of orange peel (from 1 small orange)
4 whole cloves
2 teaspoons vanilla extract

1 14-ounce can sweetened condensed milk
1½ teaspoons Tabasco sauce
2 cups heavy cream, whipped
Cinnamon sticks and orange peel twists for garnish

In a small saucepan over medium heat, heat the milk, cinnamon stick, orange peel, and whole cloves to boiling. Reduce the heat to low; cover and simmer 5 minutes to blend the flavors. Set aside to cool to room temperature. Strain the mixture.

In a large bowl, combine the milk mixture, vanilla, sweetened condensed milk, and Tabasco sauce. Gently fold in the whipped cream. Cover and freeze until firm, stirring once.

To serve, scoop the ice cream into glasses or dessert dishes. Garnish with cinnamon sticks and orange peel twists, if desired. *6 servings.*

APPLE LASAGNE

There is a precedent for a sweet noodle dessert in Jewish kugel. But when a lasagne dessert recipe comes from the North Dakota Wheat Commission (via the National Pasta Association), then you know it's the result of some home economist or farmer's wife working overtime to increase the market for the durum wheat that is pasta's main ingredient.

8 lasagne noodles
2 20-ounce cans apple pie filling
1 cup part-skim ricotta cheese
1/4 cup egg substitute
1 teaspoon almond extract
1/4 cup granulated sugar

6 tablespoons all-purpose flour
1/2 teaspoon cinnamon
3 tablespoons margarine
6 tablespoons dark brown sugar
1/4 cup quick oats
Dash of grated nutmeg

Preheat the oven to 350° F. Prepare the lasagne noodles according to package directions; drain.

Spread 1 can apple pie filling in a greased 9 x 13 x 2-inch pan, slicing any extra-thick apples. Layer 4 lasagne noodles over the apples. In a bowl, mix together the ricotta cheese, egg substitute, almond extract, and granulated sugar; spread evenly over the lasagne noodles and top with the remaining 4 lasagne noodles. Spoon the remaining can of apple pie filling over the lasagne.

In a small bowl, crumble together the flour, cinnamon, margarine, brown sugar, oats, and nutmeg. Sprinkle over the apple filling. Bake for 45 minutes. Let stand 15 minutes. Cut into serving pieces and, if desired, top with a garnish made by blending 1 cup nonfat sour cream and 1/3 cup brown sugar. *12 to 15 servings.*

CHICKEN WITH 101 CLOVES OF GARLIC

This is a Gilroy (Calif.) Garlic Festival recipe contest exaggeration of the traditional French Provençal dish, chicken with forty cloves of garlic. Contestant Helen McGlone increased the serving size to party proportions and hence also upped the already impressive amount of garlic used.

I recommend inviting guests into the kitchen to count the garlic cloves before you put it in the oven. That will increase their amazement at how mild, tender, and buttery it all turns out.

10 whole chicken breasts, split, boned, and skinned
Salt and pepper

2 cups champagne
101 unpeeled garlic cloves

Preheat the oven to 350° F.

Place the chicken in an ungreased baking pan, 12 x 16 or 18 inches. Sprinkle with the salt and pepper and pour the champagne over. Place the garlic cloves around and between the chicken pieces. Cover the pan with foil and bake for 1½ hours. Remove the chicken to a large serving platter and place the garlic around the chicken.

To eat, squeeze the buds of garlic from their husks and onto your chicken or, depending on the crowd, directly into your mouth. *20 servings.*

GARLIC ICE CREAM

For some years now, some of America's stinkiest cooking has taken place at California's Stinking Rose restaurants. Except for a small section of the menu entitled "Vampire Fare," every dish at these San Francisco and Los Angeles restaurants is seasoned with garlic. The company actually sees it as seasoning their "garlic with food."

Here's a recipe for the grand finale to any Stinking Rose meal.

3 cups whole milk	**MOLE SAUCE**
¼ teaspoon freshly chopped garlic	4 tablespoons (½ stick) butter
1 vanilla bean, split in half	1 1-ounce square unsweetened
1 cup heavy cream	chocolate
1½ cups sugar	1 cup sugar
9 egg yolks	4 tablespoons chili puree or paste

Put the milk, garlic, and vanilla bean in a saucepan. Bring to a boil and remove from the heat. In a mixing bowl, blend the cream, sugar, and egg yolks. Strain the scalded milk mixture into the egg and sugar mixture, stirring constantly.

Return the combined mixture to the pan and stir continuously over moderate heat until it coats the back of a spoon, about 10 to 15 minutes. Cool in an ice bath. Freeze until firm. Serve topped with mole sauce. *4 to 5 servings.*

To make Mole Sauce: Melt the butter and chocolate in a saucepan over low heat. Then mix in the sugar until dissolved. Add the chili puree or paste and blend until smooth. Pour the hot sauce over the ice cream.

ONION SANDWICHES

Food giant James Beard invented these sandwiches when he was still a caterer. Before you say, "Now I understand why he became a food writer," be advised that these Onion Sandwiches were actually very popular.

Although Beard served them as hors d'oeuvres, they'll probably be more conversation provoking at the center of a luncheon or tea spread.

1 1-pound loaf thin-sliced white or
   brown bread (or get a loaf of
   brioche or challah and slice it
   yourself)

1 large red onion, cut into about 20
   very thin slices
¾ cup mayonnaise
¾ cup finely chopped fresh parsley

Use a cookie cutter to cut the bread into 2-inch rounds (or use precut deli rye cocktail bread). Cover half the rounds with a single onion slice and a thin coating of mayonnaise. Top with the remaining bread rounds.

Coat the edges of each sandwich in mayonnaise, then roll them in parsley thick enough so the edges look green. Put the sandwiches on a serving plate, cover with plastic wrap, and refrigerate for at least an hour. *Makes 15 to 20 sandwiches.*

SPAM MOUSSE

"Spam speaks any language—and with such sparkle!" enthused Margaret Fulton in the Spam International Cookbook supplement to the May 11, 1970, edition of *Woman's Day* magazine.

The following "very French" recipe was inspired by a mousse in that supplement—one of several attempts by Spam-maker Hormel to glamourize its famous (infamous?) luncheon meat.

1¼ cups chicken broth
1 tablespoon plain gelatin powder
¼ cup sherry
1 tablespoon finely chopped onion
1 12-ounce can Spam, ground or finely
   chopped

¼ cup grated celery
1 cup whipped cream
Lettuce (optional)
Stuffed olives (optional)
Sliced hard-boiled eggs (optional)

Pour ½ cup of the chicken stock into a saucepan, then sprinkle in the gelatin. Let sit 2 minutes, then stir over low heat until the gelatin is dissolved. Remove from the heat, then stir in the sherry, the rest of the chicken broth, and the onion. Chill until it is the consistency of unbeaten egg whites.

Add the Spam, celery, and whipped cream. Moisten a lightly greased mold or souffle dish with cold water, then fold the mixture in. Chill until firm.

Unmold and, if desired, garnish with lettuce, stuffed olives, and sliced hard-boiled eggs. *6 servings.*

PRETZEL CHICKEN

I assumed this dish had come out of the corn flake and instant potato school of oven-fried chicken—until I had some wonderful pretzel-encrusted swordfish at a trendy bistro named Gary's Little Rock Cafe just outside of Atlantic City, N.J.

But whether it's down-home or upscale, pretzel coating is still weirdly delicious. This recipe is courtesy pretzel-maker Snyder's of Hanover.

5 to 6 Snyder's of Hanover or other large hard sourdough pretzels (yielding 1½ cups crumbs)
Salt and pepper
Pinch of sugar
Onion powder

Garlic powder
Parsley
1 whole chicken, skinned or unskinned, cut into pieces
1 12-ounce can evaporated skim milk

Preheat the oven to 400° F.

Crush the pretzels to make crumbs. Add the salt and pepper, sugar, and remaining spices to taste.

Dip the chicken pieces in the evaporated milk, then roll in the pretzel crumb mixture to coat. Bake in an ovenproof dish for 40 to 50 minutes or until meat can be easily pulled off the bone with a fork.

PIECRUST OF CHAMPIONS

Traditional fatty piecrusts are not the food of champions. That doesn't mean your home training table must be devoid of pie—at least, not if your piecrust is made of the healthful and deliciously unexpected Wheaties.

Please note: This is my own recipe, inspired by a piecrust made of the more prosaic Kellogg's Corn Flakes. If you don't like it, Wheaties maker General Mills should not be blamed.

4 cups Wheaties, pulverized down to
   1 cup
2 tablespoons sugar

2 tablespoons (¼ stick) butter,
   softened
2 tablespoons light corn syrup

Preheat the oven to 350° F.

Mix all the ingredients together in a bowl. Press the mixture onto the bottom and sides of a 9-inch pie plate. Bake 5 minutes.

The cooled piecrust can be filled with ice cream or pudding and topped with fruit slices and/or Cool Whip.

SPROUT CHIP COOKIES

Eat your vegetables! Moms could probably stop saying this forever if they served vegetables in this kind of cookie packaging.

Sprout Chip Cookies were a featured treat of the 1987 edition of the Brussels Sprout Harvest Festival held at the Santa Cruz, California, boardwalk along with the equally strange if not stranger sprout water taffy, sprout cotton candy, sprout ice cream, sprout nachos, and candied sprout-on-a-stick. Perhaps not surprisingly, this celebration no longer takes place.

Fresh brussels sprouts, parboiled,
  drained, and chopped to fill about 1
  cup
½ cup (1 stick) salted butter or
  margarine, softened
½ cup granulated sugar
½ cup dark brown sugar
½ teaspoon vanilla extract

1 egg
1¼ cups all-purpose flour
½ teaspoon baking soda
½ teaspoon baking powder
¼ teaspoon salt
1 cup semisweet chocolate baking bits
  and/or chopped nuts

Preheat the oven to 375° F.

Cook the sprouts, covered, in 1 inch of boiling water for 5 minutes. Drain, chop, and set aside. Cream together the butter or margarine and sugars. Add the vanilla and egg. Gradually add the remaining ingredients and mix until well-blended.

Drop the dough by rounded teaspoonfuls about 2 inches apart onto an ungreased cookie sheet. Bake 8 to 10 minutes, or until the edges are brown and the cookies are firm to the touch. Remove from the cookie sheet after a few minutes and cool on a baking rack. Store in an airtight container. *Makes about 3 dozen cookies.*

GHOST OF ELVIS SANDWICH

This sandwich would be pretty weird even if it wasn't one of Elvis's favorites. Elvis loved peanut butter and banana sandwiches so much that he reportedly once lived on them, and only them, for 7 weeks. For maximum authenticity, play "Love Me Tender" while making this sandwich and eat it the way Elvis did: with a knife and fork.

3 to 4 tablespoons chunky-style peanut
  butter
2 slices of Wonder Bread

1 banana, sliced
2 tablespoons margarine

Spread the peanut butter on both slices of bread, dot with the banana slices, then put the 2 slices together. Butter the outsides of the sandwich with margarine. Put in a pan and grill on the stovetop until brown. *Serves 1 Elvis fan.*

MOVIE THEATER LOBBY LOAF

Here's a great way for movie theater popcorn stand workers to help save the environment: Instead of throwing out leftover popcorn, bring it home and fashion it into a meatloaflike dinner entrée.

This recipe's enthusiastic all-popcorn cookbook source (Larry Kusche's *Popcorn Cookery* published 1977) actually positions this as a roast substitute and so recommends serving it with "your favorite sauce or gravy."

2 cups bread crumbs
$\frac{1}{2}$ cup chopped nuts (pecans or your
  favorite)
$\frac{1}{2}$ cup medium-ground popped
  popcorn
$\frac{1}{2}$ cup (1 stick) butter, melted

$\frac{1}{2}$ teaspoon instant minced onion
$1\frac{1}{2}$ teaspoons salt
$\frac{1}{4}$ teaspoon pepper
1 egg, beaten
$\frac{1}{4}$ cup or less butter, melted

Preheat the oven to 350° F. Butter a small mold or loaf pan.

Thoroughly mix $\frac{1}{2}$ cup hot water with all the remaining ingredients except $\frac{1}{4}$ cup butter. Place in the pan and bake 1 hour. Cover the pan the first 15 minutes, then baste 3 times with the melted butter. Turn out into a hot dish and serve with your favorite sauce or gravy. *4 servings.*

POPCORN SOUP

Native American Indians reportedly made a popcorn soup but I was unable to find one of their recipes. The closest I came was a recipe for a popcorn-thickened soup in *Crazy for Corn* whose only historical claim was to the evening author Betty Fussell found herself hungry for soup on a night when her refrigerator contained nothing but peppers, clam juice, milk, and some leftover popcorn.

Her recipe inspired this hearty ham soup, with popcorn serving as both thickener and garnish.

¼ cup unpopped popcorn (2 cups popped)
2 cups milk
1 cup chicken broth
1 red bell pepper, cleaned, seeded, and finely chopped
1 small onion, finely chopped
½ cup finely chopped celery
Butter
½ cup finely chopped cooked ham
Pepper to taste

Pop the popcorn, then set 1 cup aside. Place the other cup in a blender or food processor and process until the corn is pulverized. Add the milk and chicken broth and process until liquefied. (Adjust the thickness and richness of your chowder by adding more milk or broth.)

Sauté the pepper, onion, and celery in the bottom of a soup pot with a little bit of butter until slightly brown. Strain the popcorn liquid into the same saucepan, then add the cooked ham.

Simmer for about 30 minutes, or until the vegetables are soft, stirring frequently to make sure the milk doesn't burn. Serve in soup bowls garnished with the reserved popcorn and ground pepper. *3 to 4 servings.*

DOUGHNUT PUDDING

Here's a bread pudding that starts with something much more unusual, filling, and delicious than plain old bread.

3½ cups stale plain doughnuts or
   crullers, broken up and loosely
   packed
3 cups milk

3 large eggs, beaten
⅓ cup sugar
½ cup raisins
½ teaspoon cinnamon

Preheat the oven to 350° F.

Grease a 2-quart baking dish, then place the broken doughnuts in it. Combine the milk, eggs, sugar, raisins, and cinnamon in a bowl, then pour over the doughnuts. Let sit at least 10 minutes.

Half fill a larger baking dish with nearly boiling water, then set the doughnut pan into it, place in the oven, and cook until the center is set, about 35 or 45 minutes.
4 to 6 servings.

BBQ JELL-O

When you get down to essentials, Jell-O is basically the glutinous matter from animal bone, skin, and connective tissue combined with sugar and flavorings.

As if that isn't strange enough, here is a recipe for turning a sweet lemon Jell-O dessert into the savory essence of an outdoor barbecue.

1 3-ounce package lemon Jell-O
1 cup your favorite barbecue sauce

Mixed salad greens

Grease an 8 x 8-inch square pan. Dissolve the Jell-O in ¾ cup boiling water, then let cool to room temperature. Mix the barbecue sauce into the Jell-O and pour into the pan. Chill until firm. Cut into cubes and serve atop salad greens. *6 servings.*

TIPSY TWINKIES

Cooking with Twinkies isn't exactly weird (especially to anyone who grew up in the sixties), but it is fun, especially when the plebeian snack cake is used to make an elegant English dessertlike trifle.

*2 3-ounce packages instant vanilla
   pudding
6 Twinkies
4 tablespoons sherry or rum*

*½ cup raspberry, strawberry, or your
   favorite flavor jam or jelly
1 8-ounce container Cool Whip
Chopped walnuts*

Prepare the pudding according to package directions.

Put 1 Twinkie aside. Unwrap and cut 5 Twinkies in thirds lengthwise and use just enough to cover the bottom of an 8 x 8-inch or similar-sized round casserole dish in a single layer. (If you use a round dish, you may also have to cut some of the Twinkies widthwise to get them to fit.)

Sprinkle with 1 tablespoon sherry or rum, then cover with thin layers of the preserves, pudding, and Cool Whip. Repeat until you run out of food (or height in your dish), ending with a layer of Cool Whip. Cover and chill at least several hours before garnishing with nuts and, if desired, 1 uncut Twinkie. *4 to 6 servings.*

VELVEETA FUDGE

This is a legendary recipe of unknown origin and questionable wisdom. At first it tastes like fudge, then the Velveeta smacks you in the face and you say to yourself, "Good butter and chocolate and confectioners' sugar really deserve better."

½ cup (1 stick) salted butter
4 ounces Velveeta cheese
1 1-pound box confectioners' sugar, sifted

2 1-ounce squares baking chocolate, melted
½ teaspoon vanilla extract
½ cup chopped walnuts (optional)

Place the butter and cheese in a heavy saucepan and melt over low heat until smooth, stirring constantly. Remove from the heat. Mix in the remaining ingredients one at a time. Spread into an 8-inch-square greased pan and cool until firm. Cut into squares and store covered. *Makes about 1½ pounds.*

GRANOLA FONDUE

Is there anything that said sixties America like granola? That combination of fruit, nuts, and whole grains was once considered the epitome of health food. But today's fat and calorie-conscious healthy eating advocates consider it to be little better than candy.

Granola's good taste is only one reason to make this blast from our hippie past. The other is for the chance to chuckle at this attempt to meld sixties health food radicalism with that most conventional of fifties suburban entertaining vessels, the fondue pot. The recipe is from *The Granola Cookbook*.

French bread, celery, carrot, green
   pepper, and/or apple
1/2 cup (1 stick) butter
3 tablespoons whole wheat flour
1/2 teaspoon sea salt
1/2 teaspoon pepper

2 minced garlic cloves
2 cups milk
5 egg yolks, slightly beaten
1/4 cup granola
3/4 cup grated Parmesan cheese

Cut the bread and vegetables into bite-sized pieces to use as dippers. Cut the apples last, just before serving so they won't turn brown! Set aside. Melt the butter in a saucepan, add the flour, and stir until frothy. Add the salt, pepper, garlic, and 2 cups milk. Cook, stirring constantly, until thick.

Pour a small amount of the sauce into the egg yolks, stirring constantly. Pour the egg mixture into the rest of the sauce and stir about 2 minutes, or until thickened.

Stir in granola, then the cheese, and heat until the sauce is thick enough to coat the food pieces without dripping. Serve in a fondue pot with dippers. *6 servings.*

4

FLORA AND FAUNA

Americans are used to buying their food neatly packaged in cardboard or wrapped in plastic. Even if the food is as weird as fried clams or lima beans, the ordinariness of their packaging and sales venues help us to forget and accept.

But there is a great wild and wooly world of food out there beyond the supermarket checkout stand that this chapter means to introduce. We are talking about wild plants and flowers and weird animals and animal parts that are perfectly fine to eat but rarely seen that way, at least here in the US of A.

Grossness is one reason given for that omission. But is that really a good excuse considering that Americans have absolutely no problem eating bee vomit (honey) or boiled bones (gelatin)?

Convenience and availability might have been an issue fifty years ago but not now when even wild boar meat is available via overnight mail to anyone with a credit card and phone. (See the source section at the back of the book for help in obtaining some of the more unusual ingredients mentioned in this chapter.)

So what IS the problem?

When it comes to diet, we Americans are a bunch of unadventurous scaredy cats, at least compared to Native Americans and pioneers, who regularly ATE bobcat.

Animal rights activists, listen up: I am not here suggesting anyone eat their kitty cat. What I am suggesting is that there are lots of alternatives should you get bored eating hamburgers and hot dogs, with or without "cats"-up.

CHOCOLATE CRICKET TORTE

With the exception of downed pilots, insect eating has never really caught on with Americans the way it has with Mexicans (who consider caterpillars a delicacy) or Thailanders (who love giant water bugs almost as much as we love Twinkies). This, despite the fact that bugs can't hurt you and are actually high in protein and such important vitamins and minerals as zinc, iron, riboflavin, and niacin.

People brave enough to try eating insects have described them as tasting like everything from shrimp to wood chips. To help them out a bit, insects are frequently fried or enveloped by chocolate as in this dessert torte served at the New York Entomological Society's one hundredth-anniversary, $65-a-plate soiree in 1992.

1 pound (4 sticks) salted butter
4 ounces unsweetened chocolate
12 ounces semisweet chocolate
8 eggs, separated

1 cup sugar
1 cup strong coffee
2 cups crickets, toasted and roughly
  chopped

Preheat the oven to 350° F. Butter and flour an 8-inch springform pan.

Melt the butter and chocolate in a heatproof bowl placed over a pot of simmering water. Let cool to room temperature, then whisk together with the egg yolks, sugar, and coffee until well combined.

Fold in the crickets. Whip the egg whites until stiff and fold into the chocolate mixture. Bake for 30 to 40 minutes (the center will still be moist). Allow to cool 10 minutes before removing from the pan. *10 to 12 servings.*

NOTE TO PREPARE THE CRICKETS: place them in a box with a few slices of apple, pear, or leafy vegetables at room temperature for about twenty-four hours.

Several hours before you'd like to handle them, place the box in the refrigerator to slow their movements down. (They can also be put in the freezer for a few moments to achieve the same effect, or frozen solid for later use.) Once cooled, pick out and throw away the dead (i.e. spoiled) crickets and clean the live ones by rinsing in a colander. Place on a cookie sheet in a 200° F oven for 1 to 2 hours, or until the crickets are dry.

RICE FIELD SKEETER PILAF

Granted, the rangers at Crowley's Ridge State Park could probably have come up with a better name for the park's annual Mosquito Awareness Weekend. I mean, who ISN'T aware of mosquitos on a hot summer's evening, especially in a state park? Still, you've got to give the Walcott, Arkansas, event credit for being one of the few places in the world where the twin arts of mosquito calling and cookery are evaluated and honored in competition.

All cooking entries must contain at least ¼ cup mosquitos—for some strange reason, the exact amount of mosquitos this recipe from Libby Lancaster and many other entries seem to contain.

1 cup rice, rinsed

1 13¾-ounce can beef broth

1 4-ounce can mushroom pieces,
  drained

¼ cup mosquitos

Preheat the oven to 350° F.

Combine all the ingredients in a casserole with a lid and bake for 45 minutes, or until the rice is tender. *3 servings*.

TO HARVEST AND PREPARE MOSQUITO MEAT FOR SAFE EATING: Wave a fine-mesh net through any mosquito problem area rapidly and in a figure eight motion; then immediately crush the mosquito-containing net to keep the mosquitos from flying away. Bake mosquitos on a cookie sheet at 325° F for at least 20 minutes. The mosquitos can be used immediately or frozen for later use.

EARTHWORM OMELET

Have you ever wondered what fish see in earthworms? Surely they are not acting on such rational information as earthworms' protein content (more than a T-bone steak) or their economy as a food source (free for the taking and they contain no bone or gristle). But YOU can eat them for these good reasons.

The following recipe was inspired by an entry in an earthworm recipe contest sponsored by North American Bait Farms, Inc., of Ontario, California.

¼ cup chopped green pepper

¼ cup chopped scallions

1 teaspoon plus 1 tablespoon butter

3 large eggs, at room temperature

⅛ teaspoon dried tarragon

⅛ teaspoon salt

¼ teaspoon pepper

⅓ cup shredded cheddar cheese

½ cup fresh earthworms, prepared

2 tablespoons medium-hot to hot salsa

In an 8-inch nonstick pan, sauté the green pepper and scallions in a teaspoon of butter. Remove the vegetables from the pan and set aside in a small bowl with the prepared earthworms (see instructions below).

Whisk the eggs in a small bowl, then mix in the tarragon, salt, pepper, and cheese. Add rest of butter to the saucepan set on high until the butter stops sizzling. Pour the egg mixture in the pan all at once until the bottom sets (within seconds); then edge a spatula under the bottom so that the uncooked egg falls into the pan and cooks.

When there is no more uncooked egg on top, dump the earthworm-scallion-pepper mixture in a line down the middle of the eggs, then fold the thicker side of the filling over it. Cook an additional 30 seconds, top with salsa, and serve. *1 serving.*

TO PREPARE LIVE EARTHWORMS FOR SAFE EATING: Put them in peat moss for a day so you know what they've been eating. Boil in a mixture of water and lemon juice for about 10 minutes and drain.

Before eating earthworms as a snack, in a sandwich, or as a substitute for nuts in baking, you'll also need to bake them on a cookie sheet in a 200° F oven for 15 to 30 minutes.

SOUTHERN INSECT PIE

Make this pie or pass it by—if you're the average American, you'll still unwittingly be eating from two to three pounds of insects each year in the "regular" foods you eat.

Those brown and black specks you see in flour and bread? Fragments of weevils, flour beetles, and flour moths. Those brown spots on fruit? The tongues of tiny insects. A plate of fettuccine? It could contain up to 225 insect fragments per serving before the federal government would make a stink about it—and only then because of aesthetics. That's because insects are good for us, whereas preventing them through the use of more pesticides is bad.

This recipe for a pecanlike pie is from the American bible of insect cookery and preparation, *Entertaining With Insects*.

1 uncooked 8-inch piecrust
¼ cup (½ stick) salted butter
⅔ cup dark brown sugar, packed
2 large eggs
¾ cup dark corn syrup

¼ teaspoon salt
1 teaspoon vanilla extract
¾ cup cleaned insects of your choice
Whipped cream for garnish

Preheat the oven to 375° F.

Combine all the ingredients except the insects and beat until smooth. Stir in the insects and pour into a pastry-lined pie pan. Bake for 40 to 50 minutes, or until set and the pastry is nicely browned. Cool. Serve topped with whipped cream. *6 to 8 servings.*

NOODLES NASTURTIUM

Eating flowers can be more than just strange. If you don't know what you're doing and pick the wrong ones, it can be dangerous. Among those that ARE safe (providing they're free of pesticides or car exhaust toxins) are marigolds, daylilies, pansies, roses, and nasturtiums.

You can eat both the flowers and leaves of nasturtiums. A lot of people liken their taste to watercress or pepper. In fact, the word *nasturtium* comes from two Latin words that refer to a human's common reaction to pepperiness: *nasus,* or "nose," and *torquere,* meaning to "twist."

This salad was inspired by an olive fettuccine dish in Cathy Wilkinson Barash's informative *Edible Flowers from Garden to Palate.*

1 pound angel hair pasta or
    linguine
5 garlic cloves, smashed
4 tablespoons olive oil
2 tablespoons chopped chives

2 tablespoons chopped fresh basil
1/2 cup chopped fresh parsley
1/3 cup grated Parmesan cheese
18 nasturtium flowers, chopped
4 nasturtium flowers, left whole

Cook the pasta according to package directions. Meanwhile, put the garlic in a frying pan with the olive oil and warm over low heat for 3 to 5 minutes. Drain the pasta, then place in a large bowl and toss with everything but the whole flowers. Use those as a garnish. *4 servings.*

FLOWER CANDY

Forget M&M's and Skittles. Candied flower petals are just as colorful and sweet, and a lot less fattening. This recipe dates back to frontier days.

2 egg whites
Rose or violet petals (purchased from
    a store or through mail order,
    or grown without pesticides)

Superfine granulated sugar

Beat the egg whites with a whisk until frothy. Dip each petal into egg whites, then into sugar. Let dry on brown paper. Eat or store in an airtight container.

HEMLOCK TEA

Some lumbermen reportedly swear by the taste of this tea brewed from the needles of the young hemlock evergreen tree. To me its worth rests almost entirely in the shock value of telling people you are serving them Hemlock Tea, and having them assume you are talking about the deadly water plant.

4 teaspoons young hemlock tree needles

Heat 3 cups water to a boil. Lower the heat and add the needles. Steep for 10 minutes, then strain. Add sugar or lemon to taste. *Makes 4 cups.*

DANDELION MINI PIZZAS

Who decided dandelions were ugly and must be gotten out of lawns at all costs whereas thorny roses are beautiful and worth $25 a dozen? They're probably the same people who will then turn around and spend good money at the grocery store for vegetables not nearly as nutritious as dandelions.

Did you know, for instance, that dandelions contain twenty-five times more vitamin A than orange juice and about a third more cancer-fighting beta-carotene than carrots?

So what's the downside? Dandelions can taste awfully bitter unless they're harvested very early in the spring or are eaten with bread. Peter Gail discovered the latter secret and created this recipe while researching his book, *The Dandelion Celebration: A Guide to Unexpected Cuisine.*

2 English muffins, split
¼ cup shrimp cocktail sauce

¾ cup dandelions, cooked, drained,
and chopped
1 cup shredded cheddar cheese

Toast the muffins. Spread each with shrimp cocktail sauce (or a mixture of ketchup and horseradish). Cover with dandelions, then sprinkle with cheese. Microwave or run under the broiler until the cheese is melted. *2 servings.*

CLOVER CUSTARD

A popular song from the late 1920s recommends "looking over a four-leaf clover" but wild edible plant experts say you might also want to take a bite. Although only the mutant four-leaf kind are supposed to be lucky, the normal three-leaf kind are much easier to find. All kinds are tasty because of the nectar in their yellow flowers that makes them as popular with honeybees as they are with the Irish.

In fact, in this recipe, clover flowers actually serve as a substitute for sugar or honey.

2 cups yellow clover flowers　　　*4 egg yolks, room temperature*
2 cups milk　　　*1 tablespoon vanilla extract*
½ cup sugar

Preheat the oven to 300° F.

Clean and wash the blossoms. In a pot, heat water to boiling, lower the heat, add the blossoms, and simmer for 5 minutes. Drain the blossoms and set aside.

In a saucepan, heat the milk until warm. Place the sugar in a separate pan and melt over low heat until brown but not burned. Mix into the pot with the heated milk. Add the egg yolks one at a time, then the vanilla and clover, stirring constantly. Pour into custard cups.

Place the cups in a roasting pan or casserole dish at least half full of hot water. Bake 45 to 60 minutes, or until a knife inserted near the edge of a cup comes out clean. Cool, then refrigerate for several hours before serving. *4 servings.*

STINGING NETTLE SALAD UNPLUGGED

You probably won't need a field guide to identify this wild plant, nor to understand the origins of its name. Just give it a swat with the back of your hand and get ready for the stinging pain.

You might be wondering, though, why anyone would want to eat the dry land equivalent to jellyfish. The answer is revenge. Also because when these plants are boiled they lose their sting and taste something like bean sprouts. The trick is in getting someone else to harvest them for you.

4 slices of bacon
3 quarts stinging nettles
2 tablespoons sugar
2 tablespoons light brown sugar
¼ cup cider vinegar

Fry the bacon until done. Remove, crumble, and set aside, leaving about 2 tablespoons bacon fat in the pan. Add the nettles to a pot of boiling water and cook until tender. Drain and place in a large serving bowl.

Add the sugars, ⅓ water, and the vinegar to the pan with the bacon grease and bring to a boil. Let boil for about a minute, then pour over the nettles. Toss, add the bacon, toss again, and serve. *6 servings.*

TURTLE KEBABS

The famous turn-of-the-century chef and cookbook author Auguste Escoffier begins his recipe for turtle soup thusly: "For soup, take a turtle weighing from 120 to 180 pounds . . . " To which I might add, but not to anywhere it doesn't want to go.

Instructions in a more recent cookbook don't make preparing turtle sound much more inviting: "If you have a turtle destined for the pot, pen it for four or five days without food. When cooking day arrives, chop off the head and hang the turtle by its tail to bleed . . . "

It goes on, but being a sensitive sort, I won't.

Fortunately, today turtle meat can be purchased frozen, canned, or in soups. Unfortunately, commercial processing doesn't take away turtle's taste, which is often described in terms usually reserved for glue.

The most common (i.e., boring) recipe using turtle meat is turtle soup. Naturally we have chosen to present a more challenging preparation from the islands of the Indian Ocean. If the turtle wasn't bad enough, it also contains liver.

¼ cup lemon juice

3 garlic cloves, crushed

4 tablespoons olive oil

¾ pound turtle meat, cut into 1-inch cubes

½ pound calf liver, parboiled and cut into 1-inch cubes

3 eggs, hard-boiled and cut into pieces

¾ cup chutney

Cooked rice for serving

Place the lemon juice, garlic, and olive oil in a shallow bowl with the turtle meat cubes and marinate, covered, in the refrigerator for at least 3 hours. In a pan on the stovetop with a little boiling water, place the calf liver and cook until nearly tender. Drain and cut in 1-inch cubes.

Place the turtle meat and liver on skewers, one alternating with the other, and grill over charcoal or in the broiler until the meat is cooked through, about 7 minutes on each side. Serve with eggs, chutney, and rice. *3 to 4 servings.*

FRIED BRAIN SANDWICH

Modern parents send their kids to school with carrot sticks, apples, and other healthy foods because they are supposed to make kids perform at peak efficiency (and also because sending them with potato chips is now considered tantamount to child abuse).

But if we are indeed what we eat and if we really do want our children to succeed, wouldn't it make a lot more sense to send them to school with brain sandwiches?

Of course it would. Sometimes I think I'm the only person in this country who's using her noggin.

2 whole calf's brains (approximately
   1 pound)
2 tablespoons vinegar
1 onion
1 cup all-purpose flour
Salt and pepper to taste

1 large egg, beaten
¼ cup milk
Vegetable oil for frying
8 slices of bread
Lemon juice and/or mustard for
   serving

Soak the brains in cold water for 30 minutes; drain. Cover with 1 quart fresh water to which the vinegar and onion have been added. Bring just to a boil, then reduce the heat and simmer for 5 to 15 minutes. Drain. Plunge the brains into cold water and drain again.

Remove the outer membrane and arteries with a pointed knife. Cut the brains in half. Mix the flour and salt and pepper together and set aside. Mix the beaten egg and milk together and put in a shallow bowl. Roll the brains in the flour, then dip in the milk mixture. Deep-fry in oil until golden brown. Put one half brain on each sandwich and serve with lemon juice or mustard. *Serves 4 aspiring "brains."*

MOOSE MEATBALLS

W e've all been in a lodge or home with a moose head on the wall. Here's one answer to the question of what might have happened to the rest of it.

2 pounds moose trimmings, such as
   flank or neck
½ pound sweet sausage meat, removed
   from casings
1½ cups bread crumbs

½ cup milk
2 eggs
3½ cups jarred pasta sauce
3 tablespoons olive oil

Preheat the oven to 375° F. Lightly grease a 12 x 16-inch casserole dish.

Put the moose meat through the grinder twice. Transfer to a large bowl and then add the sausage meat, bread crumbs, milk, eggs, and ½ cup pasta sauce and mix until well blended. Form the mixture into meatballs.

Put some of the oil in a frying pan with as many of the meatballs as will fit and cook until brown, about 5 minutes. Repeat until all are finished.

Place the meatballs in the casserole dish and cover with the remaining pasta sauce. Cover the dish and bake at least 30 minutes, or until the meatballs are cooked through. Uncover and cook an additional 10 minutes. *8 servings.*

ALLIGATOR STEAK

Tailgate refers to the part of the car where the food is prepared during a pre–football game picnic. And tail is exactly what is grilled at tailgate parties of Georgia Bulldog fans prior to the annual football face-off between the Bulldogs and the Florida Gators—alligator tail, to be precise. It's a culinary metaphor for what Bulldog fans hope their team will do to the Gators out on the field.

If Gator fans are eating bulldog meat, then Bulldog fans definitely have the best of this event. For as tough as the Gator players and their animal namesake might seem, alligator tail meat is actually mild, tender, and sweet—shrimp and lobster are the most frequent comparisons made.

Here's a simple recipe for preparing alligator steaks the way they might at the Game.

1 pound alligator tail steaks   *¾ cup Italian salad dressing*

Marinate the alligator meat in the dressing for about 6 hours in the refrigerator in a covered bowl. Grill for about 3 to 5 minutes per side. *4 servings.*

HOPPERS À LA PROVENÇE

When was the last time you saw a summer day camp offer a course on frog gigging? Catching frogs with a hook and a red cloth is one of those lazy summer day activities that's become a casualty of two-career families.

But if frogs have been lost as recreation, they're still big as gourmet cuisine, especially in France, from whence this recipe comes.

6 frog's legs	½ cup sliced mushrooms
1 cup milk	1 bay leaf
All-purpose flour	4 tablespoons (½ stick) salted butter
2 garlic cloves, crushed	½ cup white wine
¼ cup diced onion	3 tablespoons heavy cream

Soak the frog's legs in the milk for 4 to 6 hours. Dry and lightly flour them. Put the garlic, onions, mushrooms, and bay leaf in a frying pan with the butter and sauté until soft, then add the frog's legs and brown. Add the white wine and simmer, covered, for 5 minutes.

Remove the frog's legs and mushrooms. Add 1½ tablespoons flour and heat another 5 minutes or until the sauce thickens. Add the heavy cream, frog's legs, and mushrooms, heat through, and serve immediately. *3 servings.*

BLOOD PUDDING

No, Dracula isn't the only one who drinks blood. So do most nomadic people. In his book, *Unmentionable Cuisine,* Calvin W. Schwabe also talks about how proper English ladies of the Victorian, pre-Geritol era would stop by the slaughterhouse for their monthly iron hit, and about the sausages and puddings commonly made with it. Even the mainstream *Joy of Cooking* gives instructions for thickening sauces with blood, and coolheaded instructions on how to obtain it.

Those lacking the skill or stomach for slaughtering can purchase blood frozen for about $9 a gallon from many butchers. What did you think that red stuff in the corners of the Styrofoam meat packages was anyway? Cherry juice?

2 cups milk
3 tablespoons sugar
1 teaspoon ground cloves
1 cup rice
½ cup pearl barley

4 cups fresh blood, beaten with a wire
    whisk
1 tablespoon dried bread crumbs
Confectioners' sugar

Preheat the oven to 300° F. Put the milk, 2 cups water, the sugar, and cloves in a pot on the stove over medium heat. Add the rice and barley and cook for about 15 minutes or until the mixture begins to thicken. Add the blood and bread crumbs and mix.

Pour the mixture into greased custard cups or muffin tins and place them in a roasting pan or casserole dish at least half full of hot water. Bake for about 1½ to 2 hours, or until a knife inserted near the edge of a cup comes out clean. Serve sprinkled with confectioners' sugar. *10 to 12 servings.*

GUINEA PIG STEW

Guinea pigs are a popular children's pet. Here's what to do if—despite all the money you spend on the cage—you decide you can no longer stand their damn squealing.

1 recently deceased guinea pig, boiled,
    plucked, and cleaned
7 tablespoons olive oil
1 onion, finely chopped
2 garlic cloves, crushed

1 teaspoon chili paste, or more to taste
    (found in Asian groceries or
    gourmet stores)
Salt and pepper to taste
1/3 cup peanut butter
2 potatoes, boiled, cut, and lightly
    mashed with a fork

After boiling, plucking, and cleaning the guinea pig, soak it in salted water for 2 hours. Dry and cut into quarters, then panfry in 4 tablespoons olive oil until brown. Reduce the heat and continue to cook until the guinea pig meat is done—no longer pink in the middle—then remove from the heat.

In a separate pan, fry the onion and garlic in the remaining 3 tablespoons olive oil until golden. Add the chili paste and salt and pepper. Add the peanut butter and potatoes and stir together with the other ingredients. Add the guinea pig pieces and cook together over low heat until warm. *Serves 1 guinea pig hater.*

RATTLESNAKE CHILI

Why is it that so many exotic meats taste like chicken? Rattlesnake meat is a case in point that makes me very glad it is available commercially. Can you imagine risking your life to kill one of these suckers only to slap your face and realize, like the guy in the V-8 commercial, that "I could have had a broiler-fryer?"

The presentation of this dish will be greatly enhanced if you call people to the table by shaking some maracas (to imitate the rattlesnake's rattle). This recipe is courtesy Hershey Foods, maker of Skinner Lone Star Pasta.

2 tablespoons vegetable oil	2 teaspoons salt
½ cup chopped onion	1 teaspoon cayenne
½ cup chopped green pepper	3½ cups (2 14½-ounce cans)
1 garlic clove, minced	tomatoes, undrained
1 pound lean ground beef	⅔ cup (1 6-ounce can) tomato paste
1 cup cubed rattlesnake meat	2 cups (6 ounces) Skinner Lone Star
2 tablespoons chili powder	Pasta

In a 5-quart saucepan or Dutch oven over medium heat, heat the oil; add the onion, green pepper, and garlic. Cook until tender but not brown; about 10 minutes. Add the ground beef and rattlesnake meat; cook until browned, about 5 minutes.

Stir in the chili powder, salt, cayenne, tomatoes, and tomato paste. Heat to boiling, then reduce the heat. Simmer about 2 hours. Before serving, add 2 cups water and return to boiling. Stir in the pasta and continue boiling, stirring frequently, 10 to 15 minutes, or until the pasta is tender. *6 servings.*

BATS AND BALLS

You guys might want to skip this one, which has nothing to do with baseball. This is just my name for a dinner of French fries and plain old fries.

As you may know, fries is the culinary term for the testicles of small to midsized male animals like lambs or turkeys. Beef testicles are commonly called mountain or prairie oysters. Both can be ordered from butchers and resemble sweetbreads in texture and flavor—although I find it hard to believe that's why they're considered a delicacy by the French, Spanish, Italians, and American feminists.

I made up that last part about the feminists, although it could very well be true.

1 20-ounce bag frozen French fries
1 pound turkey testicles
1 egg, beaten

1 cup seasoned bread crumbs
Vegetable oil for frying
Lemon wedges for serving

Preheat the oven according to the French fry package directions.

To prepare the nonpotato fries, make a slice in the outer skin of each with a knife and squeeze until the organ pops out. Discard the membrane and rinse the rest under water until it runs clear; drain well.

Place French fries in the oven so they will be done about the same time as the turkey.

Dip the cleaned fries in the egg, then roll in the bread crumbs and fry in the vegetable oil until golden brown. Serve with lemon wedges and French fries. *4 servings.*

GRILLED EEL

In Provence, France, eels are the centerpiece of the Christmas Eve meal. In Denmark, eel parties are part of the regular entertaining scene. In fact, *Edible Plants and Animals* author A. D. Livingston reports that Danes will drive miles to go to a restaurant with a reputation for serving a fine plate of eel and potatoes.

Why is it, then, that Americans in a recent survey said that the idea of eating eel only appealed to them slightly less than eating snake (their very least favorite food)?

Is it because eels are slimy, extremely oily, and live in the murky deep? They all seem like extremely good reasons not to eat eel to me, and a much better proof of American intelligence than IQs.

But here's a recipe anyway.

2 pounds fresh or frozen eel, already
skinned

½ cup soy sauce
2 tablespoons olive oil

Cut the eel into 2-inch pieces and marinate in a bowl with the soy sauce for at least an hour. Place the eel pieces on skewers, rub with the oil, and grill or broil each side until the eel begins to separate from the bone, about 5 minutes. *4 servings.*

SEAWEED SANDWICH

It's too late to decide you're not eating seaweed. If you eat ice cream, creamy salad dressing, pudding, canned frosting, milk chocolate, or beer, you already do. Seaweed's in these products in the form of carrageenan, a gel-like substance found in Irish moss.

Of course, it's one thing to eat some seaweed derivative unconsciously and another to substitute it for bacon in a bacon, lettuce, and tomato sandwich. But fans of the high-iron dulse seaweed (readily available at health food stores and Asian markets) reportedly swear by their DLTs.

¼ cup dulse
2 slices of whole wheat bread
Mayonnaise

2 to 3 lettuce leaves
1 small tomato, sliced

Preheat the oven to 200° F. Put the dulse on a baking pan and roast until crunchy, about 10 minutes.

Toast the bread and spread 1 side of 1 piece with mayonnaise. Top the mayonnaise with lettuce, tomato slices, and pieces of dulse. Cover with the other slice of bread and eat. *1 serving.*

SEA LETTUCE SOUP

The North Carolina Maritime Museum takes a mouths-on approach to teaching. Once a year staff members there attempt to teach people about no-longer-popular seafood items important in local history, seafoods commonly eaten only in other countries, and strange ways to prepare familiar seafood—all by direct experience. Delicacies such as whelk stew, glasswort pickles and hot 'n' sweet squid have proven so enticing that in 1983 the museum had to begin limiting attendance to 1,000.

The shutouts and those who don't live near Beaufort, North Carolina, can create their own Strange Seafood Exhibition with the help of the museum's *Strange Seafood Cookbook.* It not only tells you how to make Jeannie W. Kraus's recipe for Sea Lettuce Soup and many other dishes, it also explains where and how to harvest their strange ingredients.

½ cup sea lettuce	½ cup diced cooked chicken
½ cup diced onion	2 tablespoons soy sauce
½ cup chopped carrots	½ teaspoon cracked black pepper

Dry the sea lettuce by spreading it on a cookie sheet and heating in a 220° F oven for about an hour.

Boil the onions and carrots in 2 quarts water until they are tender, about 20 minutes. Break the sea lettuce into small pieces and add to the boiling water. Add the diced chicken and simmer gently for 5 minutes more.

Season with the soy sauce and pepper. Sea lettuce is naturally salty, so taste the soup before adding salt. Serve hot and enjoy. *Makes 2 quarts.*

ON HARVESTING SEA LETTUCE: Sea lettuce can be found attached to solid objects in tide pools in spring and looks like wilted lettuce. To insure freshness, only harvest sea lettuce that is attached to something. The *Strange Seafood Cookbook* says it's okay to harvest plants that have small holes in the blades because that simply means that "marine animals such as mud snails have been grazing on its blades." (That sure makes ME feel better.)

ALL-WASHED-UP OATMEAL COOKIES

L ike to try seaweed without having to mess with mud snails? Not to worry—there are many commercial seaweed harvesters who would love to get their feet wet for you—Larch Hanson of Maine Seaweed Company in Steuben being one.

Hanson has been harvesting seaweed by hand in boats stained with vegetable oil (marine paint is toxic) for more than twenty years. His company's primary objective is to "bring people to an awareness of gratitude toward the sea plants," according to one brochure. Another of Hanson's brochures actually suggests people go slow in introducing seaweed into their diets, since the plants contain a lot of salt.

No wonder Hanson also does other things to make money. They include building cradles that can be turned into a boat when the child grows up, leading workshops about deep connective tissue therapy, and running an informal bed and breakfast where guests should expect to find seaweed in their oatmeal cookies.

1 cup oatmeal, cooked and cooled
1 cup whole wheat pastry flour
½ cup raisins or currants, soaked

½ cup dulse, chopped and presoaked
Nonaluminum baking powder
  (optional)

Preheat the oven to 375° F.

Blend the oatmeal, flour, raisins, and dulse together to get a fairly stiff cookie batter (add water if necessary to achieve this). For lighter cookies, add 1 teaspoon baking powder and more water. Bake 8 to 10 minutes, or until the cookies are golden brown. *Makes about 2 dozen cookies.*

5

SPECIAL EFFECTS

Experienced home chefs go into the kitchen with certain expectations. Among them is the belief that pies don't make their own crusts, tea bags go into tea cups rather than chickens, and dishwashers are to clean up after a meal, not to prepare the meal in.

We once believed these things too.

Now we know that food can be every bit as defiant of rules and convention—and every bit as interesting—as any teenager.

So if your expectations of food up to this point are limited to being filled up, or, at the most, offering enjoyable tastes, hang onto your mixing bowl and prepare to be amused and amazed by all the unexpected ways food can be made and all the wonderfully strange things it can do.

SIZE 9W CAKE

The interesting thing here is not the graham cracker cake so much as the disposable pan you bake and store it in—one of the wackier uses for the versatile shoe box. If you need justification to try this turn-of-the-century curiosity, decorate the boxes with colored pencils or pens prior to filling and you've got a prewrapped food gift.

1 cup (2 sticks) salted butter, softened
2 cups sugar
6 large eggs, lightly beaten
3 teaspoons baking powder
½ cup all-purpose flour
1 1-pound box chocolate graham
  crackers, crushed into fine crumbs

2 cups milk
2 teaspoons rum extract
3 cups coarsely chopped walnuts
Whipped cream or confectioners' sugar
  (optional)

Preheat the oven to 250° F. Line a shoe box (including its lid) with wax paper.

Cream the butter and sugar with the eggs and set aside. Mix the baking powder, flour, and graham cracker crumbs together before slowly adding them to the butter-sugar mixture along with the milk. Add the rum extract, then the walnuts.

Pour the batter into the shoe box. Place, uncovered, on a baking sheet, making sure box does not touch oven top or sides, and bake 3 hours. Cool before slicing. Serve with whipped cream or sprinkled with confectioners' sugar, if desired. Store covered with the box lid. *24 servings.*

BATHTUB BREAD

There are people (and I count myself among them) who would consider any bread or roll not already baked, sliced, and wrapped in plastic unusual. But even those accustomed to making their own bread will probably find the submarine-like rising method used in this award winner from the very first Pillsbury Bake-Off Contest offbeat.

The "ocean" Pillsbury recommends for making this recipe, officially called No-Knead Water-Rising Twists, is a water-filled mixing bowl. But I think a scrupulously clean bathtub or sink would be a lot more amazing and fun.

*2½ to 3½ cups Pillsbury Best All
    Purpose or Unbleached Flour*
1 cup sugar
1 teaspoon salt
1 package active dry yeast
¾ cup milk

½ cup (1 stick) margarine or butter
1 teaspoon vanilla extract
2 large eggs
½ cup chopped nuts, any type
1 teaspoon cinnamon

Lightly spoon the flour into a measuring cup; level off. In a large bowl, combine 1 cup flour, ½ cup sugar, the salt, and the yeast; blend well.

In a small saucepan, heat the milk and margarine until very warm (120 to 130° F). Add the warm liquid, vanilla, and eggs to the flour mixture. Blend at low speed until moistened; beat 2 minutes at medium speed.

By hand, stir in the remaining 1½ to 2½ cups flour to form a soft dough. Tie the dough in a tea towel, allowing ample space for the dough to rise.

Place in a large mixing bowl and fill with water (75 to 80° F). Let stand until the dough rises to the top of the water, 30 to 45 minutes. Remove from the water; the dough will be soft and moist.

Grease 2 large cookie sheets. In a small bowl, combine the nuts, the remaining ½ cup sugar, and the cinnamon; blend well. Drop about ¼ cup dough into the nut mixture; thoroughly coat. Stretch the dough to about 8 inches in length; twist into the desired shape. Place on the greased cookie sheets. Repeat with the remaining dough. Cover and let rise in a warm place, about 15 minutes.

Heat the oven to 375° F. Uncover the dough. Bake 8 to 16 minutes, or until light golden brown. Immediately remove from the cookie sheets; cool on wire racks. Serve warm. *Makes 12 rolls.*

IMPOSSIBLE CHEESEBURGER PIE

Making pie crust is one of the most impossible of all culinary tasks. No wonder, then, that this Bisquick end run around the problem has proven so popular. The impossible in the name refers to the way the Bisquick sinks to the bottom of the pan during baking and forms its own pie crust.

Of all the impossible pie recipes (and there are ones for coconut, French apple, pumpkin, chocolate, lemon, macaroon, seafood, lasagne, taco, and chicken, among others), this cheeseburger one is probably the most popular.

1 pound ground beef
1 cup chopped onion
½ teaspoon salt
1 cup (4 ounces) shredded Cheddar cheese

1 cup milk
½ cup Bisquick Original baking mix
2 eggs

Preheat the oven to 400° F. Grease a 9-inch pie plate.

Cook the ground beef and onion until the beef is brown; drain. Stir in the salt. Spread in the pie plate and sprinkle with the cheese.

Stir the milk, Bisquick, and eggs with a fork until blended. Pour into the plate. Bake 25 minutes, or until a knife inserted in the center comes out clean. *8 servings.*

CONTINENTAL BREAKFAST IN AN ORANGE

Half of an orange is filled with a freshly baked cranberry orange muffin; the other half contains half an orange. It may not be EXACTLY what dietitians mean by the term "balanced breakfast," but it certainly has a symmetry.

This is a campfire idea that works just as well—but seems much weirder—indoors.

12 large thick-skinned oranges
2 cups all-purpose flour
3 teaspoons baking powder
½ teaspoon salt
½ cup sugar

1 large egg
1 cup milk
¼ cup (½ stick) salted butter, melted
¾ cup chopped cranberries
2 teaspoons grated orange rind

Preheat the oven to 375° F.

Cut the oranges in half. Choose some inconspicuous place on 1 or 2 of the orange halves from which to grate the orange rind and set the grated rind aside. Set half the orange halves aside.

Work your fingers between the meat and skin on the remaining 12 halves until you can work the meat off in one piece. (Using a spoon helps.) Rest the empty halves on the empty openings of a muffin tin or on a baking sheet.

Mix together all the dry ingredients, then all the wet ingredients plus the cranberries and orange rind in separate bowls. Then mix them together just until combined. The batter will be lumpy.

Fill the empty orange halves two-thirds full with batter. Bake for 20 minutes, or until the muffins are browned and a toothpick inserted in the center comes out clean.

Serve muffins still in the orange peel on a plate next to one of the halves containing the fruit. *12 servings.*

BREAKFAST IN THE BAG

Remember eating out of individual little boxes of cereal on camping trips—even pouring milk into them if you were careful enough opening them?

Well, this recipe for steak and eggs in a bag is similarly unpretentious but much more amazing for defying all reasonable expectations that it should start an oven fire. Brown bagging isn't just for lunch anymore.

4 brown lunch bags
2 pounds steak, about 1/4 inch thick
2 tablespoons olive oil

2 teaspoons seasoning or browning
   sauce such as Gravy Master
4 to 8 large eggs

Preheat the oven to 400° F.

Stand the bags upright. Cut the steak to fit in the lunch bag bottoms. Brush the steaks with the olive oil and seasoning sauce. Place the steaks in the lunch bags, then securely fold the bags closed so they are only about 4 inches tall. Stand them up on a baking pan and place in the oven, making sure the bags do not touch the top or sides of the stove. Cook 15 to 20 minutes.

Remove the baking pan from the oven, lower the heat to 350° F, then open the bags and break 1 or 2 eggs over the steak in each bag. Close the bags again, return to the oven, and cook an additional 15 to 20 minutes, or until the eggs are done. (The steak will also be cooked, although it will not be dark and crusty.) Bring the bags to the table and let guests tear open their breakfasts. *4 servings.*

TEA BAG–STUFFED CHICKEN

Foods with cavities beckon to be filled. It's not surprising that the folks at Celestial Seasonings thought to fill a chicken with tea bags. My version of their idea is lemon-honey flavored.

1 6- to 7-pound roasting chicken
8 Celestial Seasonings Lemon Zinger
* or other brand lemon herbal tea*
* bags*

½ cup honey
4 tablespoons (½ stick) salted butter
½ cup sesame seeds

Preheat the oven to 350° F.

Wash the chicken. Dampen 4 tea bags with a little bit of water and place inside the cavity. Put the chicken in a large roasting pan, add 3 cups water and the remaining tea bags to the pan, then cover the whole thing with foil. Bake 2 to 2½ hours, depending on the chicken size.

About 30 minutes before the chicken should be done, combine about a cup of the chicken pan drippings in a saucepan with the honey, butter, and sesame seeds and bring to a boil on the stove, stirring constantly. Glaze the chicken with this frequently until it is done. Serve the chicken garnished with the leftover glaze. *7 to 9 servings.*

JELL-O POKE CAKE

The very first chocolate-covered ice cream bar was invented for a little boy who couldn't decide whether he wanted to eat candy or ice cream. Jell-O Poke Cake could solve a similar problem for people who love cake and Jell-O.

One of the most fun things about this recipe is deciding what flavors of Jell-O will look and taste best with what flavor cake. The hole stabbing will also appeal to destructive people.

1 18-ounce box cake mix that includes
   pudding, any flavor
1 3-ounce box Jell-O, any flavor

JELL-O ICING
1 3-ounce box Jell-O, any flavor
2 large egg whites
1 cup sugar
½ teaspoon cream of tartar

Preheat the oven to 350° F.

Prepare the cake according to package directions and bake in 1 9 x 13-inch or 2 8- or 9-inch-diameter pans, all greased and floured. Let cake(s) cool in the pan(s) for 15 minutes, then prick with a fork every half inch.

Dissolve the Jell-O in 1 cup boiling water. Add ½ cup cold water. After the mixture cools to room temperature, pour the Jell-O over the cake(s) evenly. Refrigerate the cake(s) for 3 to 4 hours.

If using round cake pans, dip each in warm water for about 10 minutes before attempting to unmold. Frost with Cool Whip or Jell-O Icing. *12 servings.*

To make Jell-O Icing: Mix the Jell-O with the egg whites, sugar, cream of tartar, and ¼ cup water together in the top of a double boiler.

Keeping the pan over the boiling water, beat until the icing forms soft peaks (about 4 minutes if using an electric beater, longer if not). Remove from the water and keep beating until the peaks stiffen and the frosting is of spreading consistency.

HAM AND CHEESE À LA SUNBEAM

Admittedly in modern America it will probably not be often that you find yourself in a motel or hotel without room service and nothing but a supermarket to supply you with your next meal. But when and if it does happen, and you also like grilled sandwiches, you will now know what to do.

2 slices of bread	*1 slice of American cheese*
1 to 2 slices baked ham	*2 tablespoons (¼ stick) butter*

Preheat the iron to medium. Assemble the sandwich in the usual way except butter the outsides of the bread. Double wrap the sandwich in aluminum foil with generous seams to prevent leakage. Place a towel on an ironing board. Put the wrapped sandwich on the towel and the iron on the sandwich. Lift the iron up after about 1½ or 2 minutes, or when you begin to smell toasting.

Peek inside the foil. If golden, turn the foil-wrapped sandwich over and iron the other side for another 2 to 5 minutes. (The side of the sandwich with the foil overwraps will take the longest.) *Do not at any time leave the iron and sandwich unattended. 1 serving.*

NOTE: Hot dogs can also be grilled in a similar manner if you split them in half and grill their buns separately.

RABBIT HOLE CAKE

This brownielike chocolate cake is commonly called wacky or crazy cake, because it eschews such common cake-making conventions as dairy products, a mixing bowl, or greasing the pan. My name for it honors the three holes or burrows that must be made to add the vinegar, vanilla, and oil.

1½ cups all-purpose flour
1 cup sugar
1 teaspoon baking soda
½ teaspoon salt
3 heaping tablespoons unsweetened
  cocoa

1 teaspoon vanilla extract
1 tablespoon vinegar
6 tablespoons vegetable oil
Whipped cream or ice cream
  (optional)

Preheat the oven to 350° F.

Combine the dry ingredients and put into an ungreased 9-inch-square baking pan. Make 3 holes or wells in the dry ingredients.

Put the vanilla in one hole, the vinegar in another, and the oil in the third. Pour 1 cup cold water over all and mix well (the batter will still be a bit lumpy).

Bake for 30 minutes, or until a toothpick inserted in the center comes out clean. Frost or serve with whipped cream or ice cream, if desired. *6 to 8 servings.*

SALMON DIRTY DISHES

Run the dishwasher and cook dinner simultaneously. This popular underground idea is one of the few special effects recipes that actually saves time and energy. The resulting fish looks and tastes poached.

4 salmon fillets, approximately
    7 ounces each
⅓ cup chopped fresh chives

3 sprigs of fresh tarragon
Salt and pepper to taste
1 lemon, cut in half

Cut aluminum foil into 4 pieces large enough to wrap the fillets amply. Lay the fillets on the foil, then decorate each with chives, tarragon, salt and pepper, and a tiny bit of lemon juice.

Wrap each fillet up in foil, folding over the edges so they are airtight. Then wrap in another piece of foil. (Vigilance in wrapping is essential to avoid soapy-tasting fish or fishy-smelling dishwasher!)

Place on the top rack of the dishwasher with a dirty load, add the detergent, then run through the wash-and-dry cycle as usual. *4 servings, complete with clean serving plates.*

BLOOMING FUN BREAKFAST EGGS

Everyone knows about dandelions' usefulness as a butter-liking meter (if your chin develops a yellow shine when you put a dandelion flower under it, it means you like it), the way its flowers and stems can be made into chains and necklaces, and how blowing on its fluffy white seeds can make your dreams come true.

Now add this to the list of fun you can have with dandelions: making eggs with dandelion buds that bloom into flowers in the pan. Yes, you have the power to make flowers bloom even if you DON'T look like Julia Roberts.

4 eggs
2 tablespoons milk or cream
Salt and pepper to taste
2 tablespoons (¼ stick) butter

1⅓ cups dandelion buds, stemmed,
washed, and towel dried
4 dandelion flowers

Whisk the eggs and milk or cream together with the salt and pepper in a small bowl. In a saucepan over medium heat, melt the butter. Add the dandelion buds and cook until they open into flowers. Then add the eggs to the pan. Cook until the eggs are of the consistency you like. Serve garnished with the dandelion flowers. *2 servings.*

METAMORPHOSIS DESSERT

What's that you say? The only thing you have in the house for dessert is chocolate wafer cookies but you really feel more like devil's food cake? Not a problem if you have this Nabisco test kitchens recipe, some whipped cream, and the three or four hours needed for the cream to work its magic in your refrigerator.

1 cup heavy cream
2 tablespoons sugar
½ teaspoon vanilla extract

20 Nabisco Famous Chocolate Wafers
Red candied cherries (optional)

Whip the cream with the sugar and vanilla until stiff. Spread the wafers with part of the cream. Put together in stacks of 4 or 5. Chill 15 minutes. Join the stacks with additional cream to make 1 long roll. Frost the outside of the roll with the remaining cream. Refrigerate at least 3 hours.

Garnish with red candied cherries, if desired. Cut diagonally at a 45-degree angle, to create 6, ¾-inch zebra-striped slices and 2 triangular-shaped end "runts."

NOTE: The roll may be frozen. If so, remove from freezer to refrigerator about 1 hour before serving.

SOCK COFFEE

Here's a solution to the problem of waking up in a summer cabin rental that contains only a campfire-style coffee or tea pot. Who wears socks in the summer anyway?

7 tablespoons ground coffee   Old-fashioned coffee or tea pot
1 clean sock

Put the coffee into the sock. Put 6 cups of water in the pot. Tie the top of the sock closed and lower it into the pot. Put on the lid and cook until done. *Makes 6 cups.*

WATERMELON-BAKED CHICKEN

Hawaiians think the show is as important as the eats, judging from their luaus and this crazy, energy-incorrect way of cooking chicken.

1 very large watermelon   1 teaspoon jerk seasoning powder
1 lime   Salt and pepper to taste
1 roaster chicken, about 5 pounds   1/4 cup cream of coconut
4 tablespoons fresh cilantro leaves   Hot cooked rice

Preheat the oven to 400° F. Stabilize the watermelon by cutting a 1/4-inch slice off the bottom rind horizontally. Cut the top third of the watermelon off horizontally, then scoop enough of the pulp and seeds from both the top and bottom halves to fit the chicken.

Prick the lime with a fork and place inside the chicken. Also sprinkle the cavity with 1 tablespoon cilantro and some salt and pepper. Sprinkle the rest of the cilantro and all of the jerk seasoning powder on the outside of the chicken.

Place the chicken in the melon, put on the top, and secure it closed with skewers. Bake 2 hours. Reduce the tempreature to 300° F and cook another 2½ hours.

Show the whole thing to guests (or else what's the point?) before removing the chicken and ladling the watermelon juice into a saucepan. Heat until thickened. Add the cream of coconut and spoon over the chicken pieces. Serve with rice and pieces of watermelon. *8 servings.*

INDOOR S'MORES

Here's a microwave version of this classic Girl Scout campfire treat that offers the fun of watching the marshmallow grow like The Blob without the usual camp drawbacks of mosquitos and the need to sing "Kumbaya."

1 plain chocolate bar   *2 marshmallows*
4 graham crackers

Put half the chocolate bar on top of a graham cracker and top with 1 marshmallow. Microwave on high for 15 to 30 seconds, or until the marshmallow starts to grow. Top with a second graham cracker, squish, and eat. Repeat. *Makes 2 snacks.*

HALF-BAKED COOKIES

These meringue cookies start cooking right at the point when most others would be done: when you turn the oven off. Then they must sit there in an unopened oven for at least six hours.

If this isn't a weird recipe, I don't know what is.

2 egg whites, at room temperature
½ cup sugar
1 teaspoon vanilla extract

½ cup chopped nuts, any variety
½ cup chocolate chips

Preheat oven to 350° F.

Beat the egg whites and gradually add the sugar, continuing to beat so the egg whites don't lose any volume and are very stiff. Fold in the vanilla, nuts, and chocolate chips.

Cover a cookie sheet with aluminum foil or brown paper and drop the cookies by teaspoonfuls onto it. Place the cookies in the oven, then immediately turn the oven off. Let them sit for at least 6 hours before opening the oven door. *Makes 2 dozen.*

ICE CREAM COLD FEET

A kid's job is play, the child development experts say. But isn't it great when their play can be channeled into something truly useful, as in this kick-the-can ice cream–making game?

1 cup half-and-half
1 cup whipping cream
¼ cup sugar
1 teaspoon vanilla extract
1 1-pound coffee can, cleaned, with plastic lid

1 3-pound coffee can, cleaned, with plastic lid
Crushed ice
¾ cup salt

Combine the half-and-half, cream, sugar, and vanilla in the 1-pound coffee can and put the lid on. Place inside the 3-pound coffee can. Pack the space between the 2 cans with crushed ice, then pour the salt over the ice. Put lid on the 3-pound can.

Kick the can back and forth with at least one other person as if it were a (delicate) soccer ball. After about 10 minutes, open the lids, scrape any ice cream off the side of the inner can, and mix with any remaining cream.

If it needs more freezing, drain water out of the 3-pound can and repack with ice and salt. Continue rolling another 5 minutes, or until done. *Makes one quart.*

NACHOS CASSEROLE A GO-GO

Microwave popcorn has gotten us used to the idea of eating hot snacks out of bags. This takes the concept to the level of a main meal.

In the Southwest, Nachos Casserole a Go-Go is called the Walkabout and is a fixture of many fairs, rodeos, and drive-ins.

2 snack-size bags of corn or tortilla chips
1 15-ounce can chili
1 small onion, chopped

¼ cup grated Monterey Jack cheese
1 small tomato, chopped (optional)
¼ cup sour cream (optional)
1 piece of lettuce, shredded (optional)

Open the bags of chips. Dump in desired amounts of the chili, onion, and cheese, place upright in a microwave, and cook on high for 15 to 30 seconds, or until the cheese melts and the chili is warm. If desired, add the tomato, sour cream, and lettuce, then eat out of the bag with a spoon. *2 servings.*

RICE PUDDING IN-A-RUSH

Creativity in convenience food cookery reached its peak during the microwave boom of the late 1970s and early 1980s. This recipe, turning leftover dinner rice and a frozen novelty into dessert, is one delicious example.

1 frozen vanilla pudding pop
⅔ to ¾ cup leftover cooked rice

3 tablespoons raisins
Pinch of cinnamon

Place the frozen pudding pop in a microwave-safe serving bowl and microwave on medium 1 minute or just until melted. Remove the stick. Blend in the rice, raisins, and cinnamon. *1 serving.*

NOTE: 1 cup ready-to-eat pudding can be used in place of the pudding pop, although it makes the recipe less of a showpiece.

SELF-FROSTING CAKE

This cake is constructed on the same principle as pineapple upside-down cake, only with a frosting "topping." The result looks for all the world like your cake was attended to by an army of sloppy oven elves armed with knives and a jar of thin chocolate frosting.

This recipe is adapted from one that General Mills test kitchens call Hot Fudge Sundae Cake—and it certainly does taste great with ice cream.

1 cup Gold Medal all-purpose flour
¾ cup granulated sugar
¼ cup plus 2 tablespoons baking cocoa
2 teaspoons baking powder
¼ teaspoon salt
½ cup milk

2 tablespoons vegetable oil
1 teaspoon vanilla extract
1 cup chopped nuts (optional), any
   variety
1 cup light brown sugar, packed

Preheat the oven to 350° F. Line the bottom of an ungreased 9 x 9 x 2-inch baking pan with 2 layers of wax paper and then grease the top piece of wax paper and grease and flour the sides of the pan.

Mix the flour, granulated sugar, 2 tablespoons cocoa, baking powder, and salt in a bowl. Mix in the milk, oil, and vanilla with a fork until smooth. Stir in the nuts, if using, then spread the batter evenly in the pan.

Sprinkle with the brown sugar and remaining ¼ cup cocoa. Pour 1 cup very hot water over the top. Bake 35 minutes. (Traditional tests for doneness will not work.)

Let cool 15 minutes, then run a knife around the edges to loosen. Invert into a large plate (one with some depth to accomodate any elfin "messiness"). Peel away the wax paper. *9 servings.*

VERY HOT HOT DOGS AND BEANS

In our too-busy, hurry-up world few people have time to prepare Christmas pudding or cherries jubilee from the usual elaborate recipes. This does not mean our culinary lives need be devoid of the glamour that comes from serving food aflame—at least, not if you know how to adapt flambé techniques to the foods of every day—such as these hot dogs and beans.

2 16-ounce cans your favorite baked
  beans
$\frac{1}{4}$ cup catsup
2 tablespoons molasses

1 tablespoon mustard
1 pound hot dogs
2 tablespoons dark brown sugar
$\frac{1}{2}$ cup bourbon

Preheat the oven to 350° F.

Dump the beans into a 9 x 13-inch flameproof casserole dish. Mix in the catsup, molasses, and mustard. Artfully arrange the hot dogs on top of the beans and sprinkle all with the brown sugar. Cook, covered, for 1 hour, then, uncovered, for another 30 minutes.

Place the casserole dish on a serving table and dim the lights. Warm the bourbon in a saucepan, avert your face, and light. Pour or spoon the flaming bourbon onto the casserole dish. *4 to 6 servings.*

FIRE AND ICE

Setting fire to foods is always impressive, all the more so when the food you are setting fire to is such a "polar" opposite to fire as ice cream.

1 quart vanilla ice cream

$\frac{1}{2}$ cup your favorite over-60-proof spirit (such as Grand Marnier or Cointreau) or your favorite lower-proof liqueur fortified with high-proof rum, brandy, or whiskey

Let the ice cream soften for easy scooping and then scoop out individual servings onto pieces of aluminum foil. (Do not freeze dishes or they could crack.)

Refreeze until rock solid. Have an assistant put these in serving dishes as you warm the liqueur in a pan. Put a flame to the pan and, after letting it burn a few minutes (and making sure there are no napkins or tablecloths in your pathway), ladle over the ice cream. *4 to 6 servings.*

NOTE: Spirits also flame well on ice cream topped with sugary chocolate or cherry syrups.

FLOUNDERING TOWARD FLORIDA

Henry Ford made campfire cooking a quaint notion. That's because virtually everyone who travels by car (and that's virtually everyone these days) also travels with a built-in stove.

I refer, of course, to the exhaust manifold, a piece of Ford's invention whose culinary possibilities are thoroughly explored in a marvelous (and marvelously titled) little book called *Manifold Destiny* by Chris Maynard and Bill Scheller.

This book comes complete with engine diagrams, discussions of wrapping techniques, and a precise explication of what will happen if you try to bake bread in your air filter housing (suffice it to say it's not good for either the bread or your car)—and I highly recommend it to aspiring automotive gourmet chefs.

This recipe is for those who might simply want to "test drive" the concept.

3 tablespoons salted butter
¾ pound flounder or sole fillet
1 lemon, cut in half

1 tablespoon fresh dill or 1 teaspoon
*   dried*
Salt and pepper

Use 1 tablespoon butter to cover the inside of 2 pieces of aluminum foil cut large enough to enclose each fillet with generous margins. Sprinkle the fish with juice from half of the lemon, all the dill, and salt and pepper. Dot with the remaining butter, then lay the fish on the foil and wrap securely by folding in at the edges. Then wrap each piece in another piece of foil and then another.

Now go outside and follow your car's exhaust pipe up to the point where it meets the engine: that's your car's exhaust manifold and one of the hottest places under the hood. Try to find a place on or near it where you can securely place or wedge in your fish packages without interfering with any crucial engine functions. (In fact, make sure of it.) Use wadded-up foil or wire if necessary.

Fillets will be done anywhere between 40 and 90 miles or 30 minutes to 1½ hours, depending on the thickness of the fish and their placement on the engine. Use the leftover lemon half to further enliven the baked fish. *2 servings.*

NO. 2 YELLOW CANDY PENCILS

A ll you people who put tooth marks on your pencils might want to try chewing on this recipe. It is a greatly simplified version of an idea in *Roald Dahl's Revolting Recipes,* which is itself based on the even more amazing candy inventions in Dahl's *Charlie and the Chocolate Factory.*

*1½ 2-ounce packages Tootsie Rolls or   12 plain new eraserless pencils
   fruit chew candies*

Place 1 piece of candy on a small piece of wax paper. Microwave on high for 25 to 40 seconds, or until the candy is soupy and pliable.

Roll the nonbusiness third of the pencil around in the hot candy, using a buttered knife to help you glob it on whatever way you want. (Do not touch the hot candy with your hands!) As soon as the candy is firm enough not to drip, stand the pencils up in a glass. *Makes 12 candy pencils.*

BREAKFAST BOWL VOLCANO

I find Fizzies tablets to be less than appetizing when used to make a drink. But as a fun food toy, it has no rival.

The following idea for turning a bowl of cereal into an active mountain range should be reserved for weekends or else the kids will NEVER get to school.

Fizzies effervescent drink tablets, any flavor
½ cup milk, juice, or other edible liquid (Who says you can only eat cereal with milk?)

¾ cup Cheerios, Fruit Loops, or other cereal with a hole

Break up the Fizzies tablet into smaller pieces. Pour a small amount of liquid in the bowl. Pile up the cereal to make a mountain. Insert a piece of Fizzies (or should we say, lava rock?) into the top piece of cereal. Sprinkle more liquid directly onto it, then stand back. Eat and repeat.

Create an earthquake by lining up some cereal, inserting a piece of Fizzies into each, then sprinkling the liquid over it. *1 serving.*

CLOTHES DRYER SHRIMP

This is an original recipe. It just goes to show the deranged path your mind begins to take once it learns of all the weird things OTHER people are doing with food.

I tried drying several other vegetables and meats, but unpeeled shrimp was the only thing that seemed tough enough to withstand the physical rigors of being tossed around a clothes dryer—at least for the short cooking time they require.

1½ teaspoons Old Bay or other favorite seasoning (optional)
½ pound extra large shrimp

Lots of aluminum foil
1 laundry hosiery bag

Sprinkle the seasoning over the unpeeled shrimp, if desired, and toss to distribute evenly. Wrap the shrimp in aluminum foil. You can put up to 4 in a package, but put them side by side rather than on top of one another. Seal tightly, then double- or even triple-wrap. (Good wrapping is essential to avoid fishy dryer syndrome!)

Place the foil packages in the hosiery bag, close, and toss in the dryer alone. Run the dryer at the high setting for 10 to 12 minutes. Peel and eat. *2 servings.*

NOTE: Because dryer temperatures vary, you might want to check 1 package for doneness at 8 minutes. You can also cook shrimp when clothes are being dried but it will take quite a bit longer.

6

FOOD ART

Real estate agents say that the key to house buying is location, location, location. Chefs will tell you the key to cooking is presentation, presentation, presentation.

Not an artist? Not a problem. There is natural color, texture, and beauty right in your cupboard and refrigerator. Unlike other artists, food artists CAN live on what they make.

Food artists generally fall into two camps: mothers trying to amuse or distract preschoolers, and four-star-restaurant chefs with nothing better to do than carve gargoyles out of grapes. The recipes in this chapter borrow from the best of both traditions, as well as from an ever appropriate interest in having fun.

And fun is exactly what you should have with these recipes: the art critics are at the gallery down the street. And food art offers at least two ways to please: what doesn't satisfy the soul should at least fill up the stomach (and vice versa).

DIRT DESSERT

This is one of the most famous of look-alike dishes popular with kids.

4 tablespoons (½ stick) margarine
1 8-ounce package cream cheese
1 cup confectioners' sugar
3½ cups milk
2 small packages instant chocolate
   pudding mix
1 12-ounce container Cool Whip

2 1-pound packages Oreo cookies
1 clean planter
Cellophane or wax paper
Gummi worms
Candy rocks
Plastic flowers
1 clean plastic or metal spade

Mix the margarine, cream cheese, and confectioners' sugar in a blender. In a separate bowl, combine the milk, pudding mix, and Cool Whip. Then combine both mixtures.

Crush the Oreos. Line the bottom of the planter with wax paper. Spread with a layer of Oreos, then a layer of the pudding mixture alternately until done, ending with an Oreo layer.

Garnish with the gummi worms, candy rocks, and plastic flowers and dish out with the spade. *15 to 20 servings.*

LAZY PERSON'S VERSION: Simply add the gummi worms and/or insects to some crushed Oreos in a cup or to some chocolate pudding mixed with crushed Oreos. Serve with a spoon.

BY THE SEA

This is an alternative to Dirt Dessert for those who prefer the ocean to the mountains.

1 3.4-ounce package instant vanilla
    pudding
Blue food coloring
2 cups vanilla wafer cookie crumbs
Shark gummi candies

Small bear-shaped cookies or crackers
Gummi Savers or Life Savers
    candies
Mini marshmallows
Paper cocktail umbrellas

Make the instant pudding mix according to package directions, except add a few drops of blue food coloring with the milk.

Spread the vanilla wafer crumbs in a large shallow plate and blue pudding next to it so that it resembles a beach. Place the shark candies and a few bears wearing Gummi Savers into the pudding.

Hide the marshmallows in the crumbs and then stick the cocktail umbrellas into them. Put a few bears nearby. Chill until ready to serve. *4 servings.*

BEARLESS VARIATION: Mix the vanilla pudding with Cool Whip, then layer with crushed vanilla cookie wafers in a spanking new sand pail, making the crushed cookies the top layer. Decorate with candy shells and pebbles.

COLORED MASHED POTATOES AU NATURAL

Bottled food dyes are a food artist's best friend—if the food artist isn't a health food fan. Those types will probably prefer to brighten up their potatoes with vegetables as in this recipe. (So THERE all you who saw our recipe for Tang Astronaut Pie and thought there was nothing in this book for them.)

½ *pound potatoes, cleaned, peeled,*
   and diced
½ *pound carrots, peas, or beets*
   (canned or fresh)

1 tablespoon butter
2 tablespoons cream

Boil the potatoes with the carrots or small beets or by themselves for 30 to 40 minutes, or until done. If using fresh peas, hull, then throw them in with potatoes during the last 10 minutes of cooking. If using canned carrots, peas, or beets, drain the can and put the vegetables in with the potatoes during the last 5 minutes of cooking.

Drain the pan, then mash the vegetables together with a masher, adding a bit of butter and cream at the end. *2 servings.*

NUTS FOR ART MODELING CLAY

Every October, as part of its annual peanut celebration, Suffolk, Virginia, sponsors what is reputed to be the world's only peanut butter sculpting contest. Contestants are given latex gloves, knives, and about twenty minutes to express themselves in a foot-square block of peanut butter clay.

"The . . . Sculpture Contest is one of our most prestigious events," notes Suffolk Festivals director Linda Stevens. And with a lineup of past sculptors that includes Mickey Mouse, Miss Virginia, and Mr. Peanut, who could argue?

Here's a recipe for (edible) peanut butter modeling material should you want to practice up for the next competition.

1 cup powdered milk (or more)
½ *cup honey*

½ *cup nonchunky peanut butter or*
   more

Mix all the ingredients in a bowl with a spoon and then with freshly washed hands until the consistency of modeling clay. (You may have to add more milk or peanut butter.) Create. If you don't like what you made, eat it! *Makes enough for 6 small sculptures.*

DESSERT DOMES

With this recipe, I mean to build a bridge of caramel cages between the fanciest New York City restaurant and the most modest dessert of packaged cookies consumed alone in your home.

A fancy restaurant's $7.50 chocolate torte is in fact these domes' usual home. But why should the rich be the only ones to enjoy the way these caramel candy cages shatter to announce the beginning of their favorite dinner course?

1 cup sugar   *Nonstick vegetable oil cooking spray*

Put the sugar and ½ cup water in a small pan over medium heat. Stir until the sugar dissolves, then increase the heat and cook another 4 to 6 minutes, without stirring, until the syrup caramelizes to a light golden color. Set the pan into a metal bowl of cold water and ice. Cool 5 minutes, or until a spoon dipped into the caramel can make firm lines. (Do not at any time let the hot caramel touch your skin!)

While the caramel is cooling, spray the inside of a small metal bowl or ladle with cooking spray. (Some people like to line the bowl or ladle with aluminum foil and then spray that.) Scoop up a little bit of the caramel with a soup spoon, then drizzle it in interesting intersecting patterns in and around the sides of the bowl. Work quickly so the caramel in the bowl doesn't harden. (If it does, reheat it.)

Trim the edges with a spoon, then carefully remove the cage (or the aluminum foil and then the cage) from the bowl and place on a plate. Place over a dessert or other food and serve. *Makes 1 bowl-sized or 3 to 4 ladle-sized domes.*

KITTY LITTER CAKE
- - - - - - - - - - - - - - - - - -

Food art for kids may be tasty, but it is rarely tasteful. I offer this one gross recipe for the eight- to ten-year-olds in the audience at the risk of causing the adults to close the book right here.

It goes without saying that this was not developed in any food company test kitchen.

1 18.5-ounce package spice cake mix
1 18.5-ounce package white cake mix
2 4-serving packages instant vanilla
   pudding mix
1 brand new kitty litter pan
Green food coloring

1 12-ounce box vanilla wafer cookies,
   crushed
6 to 10 Tootsie Rolls
Confectioners' sugar
Plastic flies (optional)
1 brand-new plastic pooper scooper

Prepare the cakes and pudding according to package directions. Crumble the baked cake into the kitty litter pan, then add the pudding and mix. Add a few drops green food coloring to 1 cup of the cookie crumbs and set aside; mix the rest into the pan.

Soften the Tootsie Rolls by placing in the microwave for 10 seconds on high and shape to resemble cat droppings. Arrange the Tootsie Rolls on top of the cookie-pudding-cake mixture, sprinkle all with green cookie crumbs, then with a bit of confectioners' sugar. Decorate with plastic flies, if desired. Serve with pooper scooper. *20 to 24 servings.*

LAZY PERSON'S VERSION: Simply put some melted Tootsie Rolls on Rice Krispies or Grape-Nuts cereal. The bible of yucky-looking food, *Gross Grub,* also offers a casserole version using cooked rice and ground sausage.

JELL-O STAINED GLASS

Jell-O is THE medium of creative cooking expression for the average amateur American chef. Rare is the church or community cookbook in America that does not showcase at least one or two new dishes made from this highly malleable, jiggly stuff.

Jell-O Stained Glass is the apparent result of one churchgoer noticing the similarity between sparkling Jell-O cubes and her sanctuary's elegant stained glass.

*3 3-ounce packages Jell-O in
    contrasting, complementary flavors
    and colors*

*1 3-ounce package lemon Jell-O
1 cup hot pineapple juice
1¾ cups Cool Whip or whipped cream*

Prepare 3 Jell-O flavors of your choice separately and according to package directions, using 1 cup boiling water and ½ cup cold water for each. Pour into separate greased 8-inch-square pans and chill until set, about 4 hours. Cut each into ½-inch cubes.

Dissolve the lemon Jell-O in the pineapple juice, then add ½ cup cold water. Keep in the mixing bowl until it starts to set (about 45 minutes). Blend the Cool Whip or whipped cream with the partially set lemon Jell-O. Fold in the gelatin cubes and pour into a greased 9-inch tube pan. Chill until firm (at least 4 hours). Unmold and cut into slices. *10 to 12 servings.*

NOTE: Interesting artistic effects can also be achieved with Jell-O through such time-honored but less time-consuming methods as ribboning (alternating different colored layers of Jell-O and/or Cool Whip), tilting (leaning half-filled dessert glasses of Jell-O against the refrigerator wall so it sets at a diagonal), and pinstriping (letting heavy cream fall into pathways created by moving a straw through some set Jell-O).

JELL-O AQUARIUM

If Jell-O Stained Glass represents the pinnacle of the adult Jell-O chef's art, then Jell-O dioramas and aquariums are the equivalent achievement among the younger set.

Gone are the days when grammar school diorama projects sit dusty on the classroom shelf long after their creators have gone on to graduate school. Today it's the lucky teacher who is able to register a grade before the floating vegetables and translucent gummy candies have been consumed.

2 to 3 4-serving packages blue Jell-O
4 to 6 ounces red hots, Nerds, or small
   candy rocks
1 new small-to-medium fish bowl
1 to 3 pieces of parsley or flowering
   kale
6 to 12 Swedish or gummi candy fish

Prepare the Jell-O according to regular, not quick-set, directions. Pour the red hots, Nerds, or candy rock gravel into the bottom of the fish bowl. Pour half the Jell-O into the bowl, then insert the greens. Refrigerate until soft-set.

Spear the Swedish fish with toothpicks and carefully insert them into the Jell-O "water." Pour in the rest of the Jell-O and refrigerate until fully set. *8 to 12 servings.*

NOTE TO LAZY PERSONS: Less elaborate individual edible "aquariums" can be constructed in clear plastic cups.

SPIDER CAKE

There are a whole bunch of recipes to put foods together to look like animals for the amusement of children. Most are unworthy of this book. But this cake's realistic filling captivates. Cut into it and it spurts out green goop just like a real spider would underfoot.

1 4-serving package green gelatin or
  pistachio pudding
1 18.5-ounce package cake mix, any
  flavor
1 16-ounce can chocolate frosting

Blue food coloring
8 black licorice sticks
Gumdrops, M & M's, or other round
  candy for eyes

Prepare the gelatin or pudding according to package directions and let it set. (If gelatin, whip well in a blender or mixer once set.) Prepare the cake mix according to package directions, except bake the cake in 2 metal bowls, one bigger than the other.

Unmold, then cut the bigger cake (to be the spider's "body") in half horizontally. Carefully scoop out holes in each half. Fill with pudding or whipped gelatin and reattach the halves.

Mix the blue food coloring into the chocolate frosting to make it black, then frost both cakes. Place the small one on top of the large one on a serving platter. Use licorice sticks as legs. Put on candy eyes. *10 to 12 servings.*

RED VELVET CAKE

I f you've ever seen this recipe before, it was probably attached to a story about a woman who paid $1,000 for the recipe for the bright red cake served at the Waldorf-Astoria hotel in New York City. The purchaser was so disappointed by the red food coloring "secret" that she took revenge on the Waldorf by handing out the recipe—sometimes called Red Devil's Food Cake or Waldorf-Astoria Cake—free to everyone and anyone who asked for it.

Folklorist Jan Harold Brunvand says this story is just as false as the similar one that crops up now and again around the recipe for Mrs. Field's chocolate chip cookies. The stories live on because they strike deep at the core of our sense of injustice and righteous revenge. But this recipe continues to be made because the cake just plain tastes good.

½ cup vegetable shortening
1½ cups sugar
2 large eggs, beaten
2 cups all-purpose flour
2 heaping tablespoons cocoa
½ teaspoon salt
1 cup buttermilk
1 ounce red food coloring
1 teaspoon baking soda

1 tablespoon white vinegar

BOILED ICING
¼ cup flour
1 cup milk
1 cup (2 sticks) salted butter
1 cup sugar
1 tablespoon vanilla extract

Preheat the oven to 350° F.

Cream together the shortening and 1½ cups sugar; add the eggs. Sift 2 cups flour, the cocoa, and salt together.

Mix the buttermilk with the food coloring and add to the sugar-egg mixture. Gradually add the dry ingredients to the wet and beat well. Add the soda to the vinegar and add to the batter.

Pour into 2 lightly greased and floured 8- or 9-inch cake pans. Bake 30 to 35 minutes, or until a toothpick inserted in the center comes out clean. Frost with Boiled Icing.

To make the icing: Blend the flour with the milk and cook over moderate heat until thick, stirring constantly until the consistency of pudding. Refrigerate until very cold.

In another bowl, cream the butter, sugar, and vanilla until fluffy. Add the cooled milk-flour mixture and beat until smooth. Spread between the layers and on the sides and top of the cake. *10 to 12 servings.*

GIANT COOKIE

An alternative to bankruptcy for Mrs. Field's fanatics: Instructions on making a cookie that should hold you for at least a week.

Enough dough from your favorite
  chocolate chip–type cookie recipe to
  yield 5 dozen regular-sized cookies

Preheat the oven to 325° F. Completely cover a 12-inch pizza pan with foil, then place the pan on a baking sheet. Grease the foil lightly, then use a saucepan cover or baking pan to trace a 10-inch circle in the grease.

Put about 3 cups of dough in the center of the circle, then spread it out so it fits neatly within your 10-inch circle. Bake the cookie for 20 minutes, then cover with foil and bake an additional 15 to 20 minutes, or until it feels barely firm at the center.

Remove from pans, cool on a wire rack, and back with cardboard to keep from breaking. Store wrapped in foil. *Makes one 12-inch cookie.*

SOUTHERN BELLE IN-A-CAKE

Perhaps you've heard of the New Orleans Mardi Gras tradition of the King Cake, a garishly decorated cake containing a plastic baby which is supposed to bring the person who finds it good luck (assuming they don't break a tooth on it, that is).

Sound like fun? Sure it is, but not nearly as much fun as shoving a Barbie or G.I. Joe into a cake up to its armpit then decorating around it in the manner of craft creatures built around spare toilet paper rolls.

The following recipe is for creating a southern belle cake perfect for a *Gone With the Wind* party but cake artists with different shaped pans and only a little imagination could create cake dioramas of Santa going down a chimney, a soldier in quicksand, and swimmers in a sea of blue frosting, floating or drowning, to give only a few examples.

1 18.5-ounce package cake mix, any flavor
1 tablespoon butter or margarine
1 plastic doll

2 16-ounce cans white, pink or other pretty pastel colored frosting
Several tubes of frosting with decorator tips
Candy decorations (optional)

Heat oven to 350° F or whatever temperature package directions say. Prepare cake according to package directions. Grease the inside of a medium, round, oven-proof bowl with the butter or margarine and fill ¾ full with batter. Bake slightly longer than directions say. Cake will be done when a toothpick inserted in the center comes out clean.

Let cake cool, then carefully unmold and dump it out of the bowl and onto a plate, flat side down. Shove a Barbie or similarly sized doll feet first into the center of the cake up to her waist. Frost the cake (and the doll's top if she's not wearing any clothes), then decorate it so that it looks like a fancy ball gown. *8 to 10 servings.*

ALL-ORANGE SALAD

As a general rule, a plate of food should always display a variety of shapes and colors. But it's fun to break the rules occasionally, as with this All-Orange Salad.

Or have even more fun by making this the opening course in an all-orange meal.

1 orange, peeled, sectioned, and cut
2 carrots, peeled and chopped
⅓ pound orange cheddar cheese,
 cut into small cubes

1 orange-hued pepper, cut into
 small pieces
French salad dressing

Assemble the ingredients in a bowl, then pour on the dressing. *2 servings.*

EDIBLE PAPER ART

Create a paper doll version of your most hated person out of edible rice paper, then play like the Big Bad Wolf and eat them up!

Or haul out a crude rice paper painting, then threaten to eat it if your friend isn't absolutely in love with it. (Of course, you don't tell her it's on rice paper.) Then watch her face when you do it!

These are only a couple of the fun possibilities presented by this paper!

Paper towels
Sheets of rice paper (sold in Asian
 markets)

Exacto knife or scissors
Brand-new paint brush (optional)
Food coloring (optional)

Wet paper towels, put the sheet of rice paper you want to work on between them, and blot until moistened but not too wet. You want the paper to attain the flexibility of latex gloves.

When it does, cut it into a paper doll or other shapes. Paint with the food coloring and/or eat, if desired.

You can also use food coloring to paint or print on dry rice paper as you would any other textured paper.

PIG NEWTONS

The concept of a savory Fig Newton look-alike could work with many different fillings but few funnier than Spam luncheon meat—in no small part because of how the word for its primary source ingredient rhymes with fig.

Mary Anne McQuillan and Fred Sterner of East Freetown, Massachusetts, were inspired to create this recipe after hearing the name in an article about a Spam cooking contest in Austin, Texas.

1 12-ounce can Spam

1 8-ounce can refrigerated crescent roll dough

Preheat the oven to 350° F.

Cut the Spam in half widthwise, then in ¼-inch slices. Unroll the rolls and separate into two long rectangles. Pat the remaining perforations in the rectangles closed.

Lay the Spam slices end to end down the middle of the dough from one short edge to the other. Bring the sides to lap over the Spam and seal with your fingers.

Turn the whole thing over, slice into 1- to 1½ -inch sections and place seam side down, on a cookie sheet so they look like Fig Newtons.

Repeat for the second piece of dough and the remaining Spam (you will probably have some Spam left over). Bake 15 to 20 minutes, or until golden brown. *Makes about 14 Pig Newtons.*

DESSERT BURGERS

Thirteen-year-old Carol Brandel of Tehachapi, California, won first prize with this McDonald's Value Meal look-alike in a recent Sara Lee contest asking kids to make objects from its pound cake.

The question is whether eating this will make you better appreciate the beauty, versatility, and deliciousness of Sara Lee pound cake or simply leave you hungry for a burger.

1 16-ounce family-size Sara Lee
 Pound Cake, frozen
2 16-ounce cans frosting, 1 white, 1
 chocolate
1 teaspoon sugar

Green and red food coloring
¼ cup shredded coconut
2 tablespoons honey, set in warm
 water to soften
1 teaspoon sesame seeds

Slice the pound cake horizontally into 3 equal layers. Cut 6 circles out of the layers (2 from the top layer for bun tops, 2 from the middle layer for burgers, 2 from the bottom layer for bun bottoms) using the plastic frosting lid as a guide.

Cut the remaining cake into ½-inch strips for French fries. Sprinkle with the granulated sugar and set aside.

To make the burgers, frost the round middle pieces of pound cake with chocolate frosting and set aside. Turn the top buns over before frosting. Spread the white frosting on the top and bottom buns to resemble mayonnaise.

Add the red food coloring to ¼ cup white frosting to resemble ketchup. Spread the red frosting over the white frosting. Place the chocolate burgers on the bottom cake buns.

Tint the coconut with the green food coloring to look like lettuce. Sprinkle the green coconut on the burgers. Add the top bun, frosting side down. Glaze the bun tops with the softened honey and sprinkle with the sesame seeds.

Arrange the pound cake burgers and fries on a plate and add a dollop of red frosting to resemble ketchup near the fries. *6 servings.*

LAZY PERSONS VERSION: Make a mini dessert hamburger by sandwiching a chocolate-covered mint or chocolate-covered peanut butter cookie patty between 2 vanilla wafer cookies.

ICE CREAM AND CAKE MIX-UP

Here's another look-alike recipe that should send anyone who is already a little bit mixed up totally over the edge.

1 10-ounce box cake mix
1 1.5-ounce box flat-bottomed ice
   cream wafer cone cake cups
1 16-ounce can prepared frosting

1 quart ice cream
Foil cupcake liners
Chocolate or colored sprinkles

Preheat the oven to 350° F.

Prepare the cake mix according to package directions. Pour the batter into the waffle cones until about two-thirds full. Stand the cones in muffin tins and place in the oven. Bake for about 20 minutes, until the batter puffs up onto the top of the cones. Frost so that it looks like soft-serve ice cream.

Put a scoop of ice cream in each cupcake liner and decorate with sprinkles. *12 servings.*

DOG BONE TREATS

Add this to the list of reasons to think America strange: At the same time as the number of people cooking dinner at home dives, pet stores report an increase in sales of cutters to make homemade dog biscuits.

The less pet-centered and more fun-loving among you can use those same dog biscuit cutters to make cookies that will fool your friends—especially if you serve them from a real dog biscuit box or beside a bowl of ice cream served in a (new) dog bowl.

1 cup (2 sticks) salted butter
½ cup granulated sugar
½ cup dark brown sugar

1 teaspoon vanilla extract
2 tablespoons milk
2½ cups all-purpose flour

Preheat the oven to 375° F.

Cream the butter and sugars together. Add the vanilla and milk and blend well. Gradually add the flour. Wrap the dough in plastic and refrigerate for 2 hours.

Split the dough in half, then roll one half out until about ¼ inch thick. Cut out with a dog bone cutter. Place on an ungreased cookie sheet ½ inch apart and bake for 8 to 10 minutes. *Makes about 24 bones.*

LAZY PERSON'S VERSION: Just eat the real dog biscuits. There's nothing in them that's really bad for you. Rye crispbread fans (admittedly not your average people) might even like them.

PUDDING PAINT

Pudding finger paint is every bit as messy as regular finger paint; the cleanup is just lots easier and more fun.

1 5.1-ounce box instant vanilla
   pudding mix
2 cups milk

Food coloring (assorted colors)
Heavy paper

Prepare the pudding mix according to package directions, except use only 2 cups milk instead of three. Divide the pudding into as many bowls as you want colors. Add food coloring.

Spread the paper out, make the kids wash their hands, and let them at it.

CHECKERBOARD CAKE

This idea is so old that it may be new to lots of people: baking a two-layer cake in which each layer contains two or three concentric rings of different-colored batter. Alternate the batters when you make the different layers and the look, when you slice into it, is of a checkerboard.

Check?

1 large piece of shirt or file folder
  cardboard
2 tuna cans, thoroughly cleaned and
  missing both top and bottom lids

1 18.5-ounce package white cake mix
1 16-ounce can white frosting
Red or any other food coloring

Preheat the oven to 350° F.

Grease 2 8- or 9-inch round baking pans. Construct 2 rings out of soft cardboard cut to about 2 inches high and 18 inches long. Hold together with tape, then wrap both in foil. Place 1 in each baking pan. Then place a coverless tuna can in the center of each pan. Prepare the cake batter according to package directions. Divide the batter in half in 2 bowls.

Dye one of the batters with a few drops of food coloring. Pour the dyed batter into the outer and inner circles of one pan and the middle circle of the other. Pour the nondyed batter in the leftover circles. Push the batter down evenly in the rings with a spatula, then remove all the cardboard and tin can dividers. Bake according to package directions.

Dye half of the frosting and frost in different squares of color, if desired. *10 to 12 servings.*

NOTE: Instead of food coloring, you can use melted unsweetened chocolate squares to create a second color with a chocolate flavor.

7

CULINARY CURATIVES

Alternative uses for everyday objects has only just recently become de rigueur in interior design. (The vision and skill to nail an old bench to the wall as a bookshelf, for instance.) But it's been a fact with food since colonial times.

How and why would it occur to someone to pour oatmeal on their hair or vinegar on their car windshield? To make spackle out of salt, or corn remover out of tea? In other words, to do almost everything with food BUT eat it?

I don't know. But that will not stop me from offering some of my ideas.

One is that this might have been a way to use up bad-tasting food; another, a case of desperation when the household product designed for the job wasn't available. And don't forget the ever-popular cheapness—because using lemon juice to do everything from clean up rust to highlight your hair will certainly save you money over buying a bunch of specialty products.

Other alternative uses were undoubtedly some product manager's idea of a way to sell more of his or her food "baby."

The vast majority, though, can probably be credited to housewives with not enough to occupy their very active imaginations, and their professional incarnations, Heloise and Mary Ann.

I salute them all and herein present some of their strangest ideas.

- -

A NATURAL HIGH

There may be something to this talk of healthy foods making you feel good, at least when the healthy product in question is shredded wheat. According to Dr. David Conning, director of the British Nutritional Foundation, a large bowl of that time-honored cereal could contain enough natural LSD (produced by a fungal infestation common to wheat) to induce mild euphoria in those not used to the drug.

1 large bowl shredded wheat cereal

Invite some friends over. Get out the cereal bowls and put on some Pink Floyd. Chow down.

A TUB OF TEA

You've heard of being in hot water. You can actually steep in it if you take tea makers' advice to save money on expensive bath oil beads by scenting your bath with your favorite flavored tea.

2 bags any flavor regular or herbal tea   *Bathtub full of hot water*
  (except ones that might leave you
  looking red or orange)

Stir, lie down, and enjoy. (In the summer it might be better to choose a regular tea as the tannic acid in it is supposed to help soothe sunburns.)

CALMING COLA

A lot of people drink cola for the pepper-upper qualities of its caffeine. But cola is also known for a seemingly contradictory ability to calm an upset stomach.

1 glass cola, warm and flat

Sip slowly at the first sign you might be able to eat or drink anything.

HOLD THE LETTUCE HAIR CONDITIONER

Some people have found the solution to a dry sandwich and dry hair in one and the same food.

2 to 4 tablespoons mayonnaise

Work into hair once a week. Leave on for 30 minutes, or until someone comes at with you with a slab of baloney—then shampoo it out.

TRAFFIC LIGHT TRAINER

Kids and dogs need rewards for learning. For years M&M's candies have served as both learning tool and reward for parents trying to teach their kids about traffic safety.

1 bag plain M&M's (only because most kids prefer them to peanut)

Teach about red, green, and yellow traffic lights with M&M candies of those colors. If your child is able to correctly relate the M&M colors to when she can and can not cross the street, let her have some to eat.

SPIT AND POLISH SAUCE

Considering that Worcestershire sauce was invented at the request of a nobleman (Sir Marcus Sandys, governor of Bengal), it seems entirely appropriate that it would be as good at polishing brass as enlivening the taste of steak.

1 bottle Lea & Perrins Worcestershire sauce

Shake some sauce onto a damp cloth and rub on brass. Polish dry.

MONKEY MASK

To answer the obvious question: No, giving yourself a banana facial does not mean you will end up looking like a monkey. On the other hand, if you decide to try this, don't encourage speculation by acting like one of these animals.

1 very ripe banana	*2 teaspoons olive oil*

Mash banana in a bowl and blend in oil. Apply to face. Leave on for 15 minutes before washing off with clear water. Pat dry.

BERRY GOOD FOR THE BLADDER

Its unadulterated flavor could, in the words of one writer, "raise blisters on asbestos." And yet its juice enjoys great popularity. One reason? Cranberry's famed ability to combat urinary tract infections.

1 glass cranberry juice

Drink once a day as a urinary tract infection preventative.

SPAM BAIT

Spam may have its detractors among the human species but catfish and carp love it—that according to the many fisherman who have caught these fish with Spam bait, including a winner of the Indianapolis *Star* newspaper's 1980 Big Fish Contest.

Star columnist Bill Scifres has speculated that these fish like Spam luncheon meat because it's "loaded with spices and somewhat oily" and catfish have "a keen sense of smell."

1 can Spam

Open can and cut Spam into ¼-inch slices. Cut the slices into strips 1½ inches long and ½ inch wide. Worm it on your hook.

PLUMBER'S HELPERS

Here are two Metamucil alternatives that, if you think about it, make perfect sense.

1 to 3 tablespoons olive oil	or	*4 tablespoons lemon juice*
		1 cup warm water
		1 tablespoon honey (combined with previous two ingredients)

Ingest either combination for relief from constipation.

THE ORANGE TANG BOWL

Tang has already proven its worth in outer space, but did you know it's also good for cleaning your home's most obvious connection to deepest earth? I mean, of course, your toilet bowl.

1 jar Tang

Sprinkle a generous amount of Tang into the toilet bowl. Let sit for 30 minutes, brush, then flush. (Or should we say blast off?)

POOR KIDS' GAK

Every generation of American kids seems to have been sold a clean mud–type toy. And with each passing generation, the toy gets more expensive. Here's a recipe for the cost-conscious glop home brewer.

½ cup cornstarch (plus)   *1 drop green food coloring*

Stir the cornstarch and ¼ cup water in a 1-quart bowl with green food coloring until the mixture is smooth and wet. Pick up the stuff and roll it into a ball. Leave it in your hand and watch it flatten and ooze. Continue to play and see it become, by turns, shiny, dull, hard, and powdery. For additional effects, add more cornstarch or water.

A NUTTY SHAVE

Conservative former senator Barry Goldwater reportedly pioneered the use of peanut butter as shaving cream. That should come as no surprise to liberals who always suspected he WAS nuts.

1 jar smooth peanut butter

Apply and shave as with shaving cream. Watch out for elephants.

FIERY FEET

"Hotfoot it" means to move quickly. But it could also be an accurate way to describe how some skiers and hunters sprinkle hot pepper in their socks to keep their feet warm.

1 pair of clean socks   *Cayenne pepper*

Get a friend to hold open your socks while you sprinkle some cayenne inside. Don the socks and go fearlessly out into the cold.

PEELIN' HEALIN'

Banana peels are the primary prop for the world's most popular sight gag. According to folk remedy experts Joan and Lydia Wilen, they can also help heal the physical and psychological damage done by falling on one.

2 ripe bananas, peeled　　　　　　*1 banana peel*

Peel a banana. Apply the inside of the peel to your grazed knee to promote healing. Peel the other banana, then eat them both. The serotonin and norepinephrine in them should help make you feel more positive about your accident—and maybe your whole life!

NUTTY GUM SOLVENT

Who among us can say they've never gotten bubble gum stuck in their hair? Only people who blow bubbles without exuberance, and who wants to do that?

But just because you've created the hairy problem doesn't mean you have to remain stuck with it—at least, not if you also have some peanut butter in the house.

1 fingerful peanut butter　　　　　*1 mass of bubble gum–enmeshed hair*

Work the peanut butter into the gum-entangled hair for several minutes. Remove.

OVERNIGHT ICE SCRAPER

If an ounce of prevention is really worth a pound of cure, then using this on your windshield at night will be a lot easier than scraping in the morning. Unless you live in Southern California (then it would be a pound of pointlessness).

¾ cup white or apple cider vinegar

Mix the vinegar with ¼ cup water and apply to your car windshield with a rag before retiring the night before a frost is expected. Sleep in to the sound of neighbors scraping.

KOOL-AID HAIR DYE

Run out of Lady Clairol or simply sick of the boring colors they offer? Try this more distinctive, less expensive alternative popular among teenage punks. (Can't you just see that frosted pitcher smile turning into a frown?)

1 to 3 packets of a single flavor of unsweetened Kool-Aid (not presweetened)

1 large bowl or bucket

Stir 1½ quarts water and the contents of the Kool-Aid packet(s) into the bowl or bucket. Pour onto and wash into bone-dry hair.

Individuals will need to experiment with which flavor and what strength Kool-Aid works best on their hair. The color is typically stronger at the end of the hair than the roots.

The color also varies in durability, but it will not wash out immediately.

COLA LAUNDRY DEGREASER

If helpful hints columnist Mary Ellen is right in believing that cola is the perfect thing to loosen stains from a load of greasy clothes, what the heck is it doing to our stomachs and intestines?

1 can cola   *Laundry detergent (usual amount)*

Put the cola and detergent into the washer with a bunch of greasy clothes.

YEAST-FIGHTING FOOD

Some doctors believe that regular consumption of yogurt containing live yogurt cultures can help ward away yeast infections. The feminist health book, *The New Our Bodies, Ourselves,* goes one step further, telling of women who claim to cure yeast infections by inserting yogurt directly into their vaginas.

1 turkey baster   *1 cup yogurt with live yogurt cultures*

You'll have to figure out the rest.

SPICE PAINT

This is art that smells as good as it looks (if you're not that good an artist, the smell may be the best thing).

Rubber cement	Assorted colorful spices such as curry,
Piece of white cardboard	cinnamon, parsley, salt, sage, black
	pepper, and cayenne

Brush rubber cement on cardboard on whatever part of the painting you want to work on first. As soon as it looks dry but still feels tacky, put a spice on your fingertip and begin "painting." Use the containers' shaker holes for a more impressionistic effect. If too much spice comes out, just turn the cardboard over and shake the excess off.

SWEET SLEEP

Ever been tempted to drug your children to get them to sleep? Honey is a natural sedative, according to Joey Green's *Paint Your House With Powdered Milk.* Green claims it can also help prevent bed-wetting.

1 teaspoon honey

Administer to a child over one year of age just before bedtime teeth brushing.

PEEL PERFUME

A medium-sized bag of fruit-scented potpourri can cost upwards of $15. Before you fork out that kind of money, you might want to check out this cheapie Morton Salt version.

| *1 orange* | *½ cup Morton Salt* |

Cut an orange in half and remove the pulp from one half without cutting the peel. Fill the empty orange half with salt. It will react with the citric acid in the orange, creating a pleasant scent.

SLUG BUSTER

Why did God create slugs? Is there anywhere on earth where they're really welcome? Is there anything that can be done about them beyond simply saying, "Yuk! Gross!"

I don't have an answer to the first question. The answer to the second and third are no and yes. The whys and wherefores follow.

Salt   *A slug problem*

Sprinkle salt on the edges of your sidewalk, near your pet dishes, or wherever else you have a problem with slugs. Watch them disappear. A saucer of beer also works well!

QUICKIE QUAKER SHAMPOO

No time to wash your hair? No need to let that oil slick on the top of your head be a lighthouse beacon to that fact—at least, not if you have some oatmeal in the kitchen cupboard.

½ cup old-fashioned oatmeal, uncooked and unflavored

Work the oatmeal into your hair with your fingers. Brush well, making sure not to leave any cereal behind to be mistaken as dandruff.

PUCKER UP, YOU PIMPLES

Pimples—once the bane only of teenagers—are today also terrorizing the father of the bride and the salesman about to make a big presentation. Here's one possible solution.

1 plastic squeeze bottle of lemon juice

Apply a drop or two to a blemish or pimple several times a day and see if they don't pucker up and go away.

OIL OF OLIVES

Here's a dry skin solution that proves that oil is oil is oil—except that the olive kind is lots less expensive than Oil of Olay.

1 bottle of olive oil

Shake onto dry skin and rub in.

UPPER FOR FLOWERS

7-Up got its name from a former ingredient—the powerful mood-elevating drug, lithium. Today's drug-free formulation is still an upper—for just-picked flowers.

1 pint 7-Up or other clear-colored,   *½ teaspoon bleach*
*   non-diet soda*

Mix a pint of water with the 7-Up and bleach in a vase and arrange flowers in it. (The sugar in the 7-Up feeds the plants; the bleach helps retard the growth of bacteria that clog the water-conducting tubes in the flower stems.)

SHOPPING TRIP REDUX NOTE PAPER

Many supermarkets encourage shoppers to reuse and/or recycle their grocery bags. But this recipe tells you how to make recycled paper from grocery bags and a few of the foods they once carried from the store.

1 2- to 3-item brown paper shopping bag or 1 large side panel from a standard-size brown paper bag, ripped into 1-inch squares

1 tablespoon dried herb or strips of orange or lemon zest left out to dry 2 to 3 hours

Place the paper in a blender. Add 4 cups water and let soak for 30 minutes. Add the herbs or zest and run the blender at high speed for about 60 seconds.

Rest a portable window screen over an 11 x 17-inch roasting pan. Pour the blender contents over the screen, letting the water drain into the pan and distributing the pulp evenly over the screen.

Put the screen on a towel on the countertop. Place a piece of folded cheesecloth on the screen and press down to force the water out of the pulp.

Lay a large baking sheet over the cheesecloth-covered screen, flip the whole thing over, then lift off the screen so the pulp is now on the cheesecloth-covered baking pan. Pat the pulp with a sponge to absorb more water.

Completely cover the pulp with a second piece of folded cheesecloth and pat down. Let dry for a minimum of 24 hours. When the paper is dry, peel it away from the cheesecloth. *Makes 1 sheet approximately 9 by 12 inches.*

RICE PACK

From relieving hunger pains to soothing muscle aches—rice is a versatile product indeed.

Fabric
Sewing skills

Rice

Cut 2 pieces of fabric to the size and shape you would like in a heating pad or medicinal cold pack. Sew 3 sides together. Fill with rice, then close up. Because rice packs cannot be washed, you might also want to make a removable slipcover for it.

For use as a heating pad, heat in the microwave for about 20 seconds. To use as a cold pack, place in the freezer for about 20 minutes.

JUST SAY NO TO SNOW TOES

Poor pooch got snow between his toes? Kid and home expert Vicki Lansky suggests spraying the problem away.

1 can nonstick cooking oil spray

1 dog

Spray the bottom of your dog's feet before he goes out in the snow and the snow won't pack between his pads.

PLAY DOUGH

This is homemade play clay very similar to the toy store kind but costing less dough because that's what it's made of.

1 cup flour
½ cup salt
2 teaspoons cream of tartar

1 tablespoon salad oil
Food coloring (optional)

Mix all ingredients but the food coloring together with 1 cup water in a saucepan. Cook over medium heat, stirring constantly until the mixture is very thick, pulls away from the kettle, and has a doughlike consistency. Cool slightly, then knead in the food coloring.

Store in airtight plastic bags or containers if you want it to stay pliable. Allow to dry to make a more permanent, claylike object and paint with food coloring, if desired.

NOTE: Although nontoxic, play dough is a toy, not a food.

8

SPECIAL OCCASIONS

Why is it that the same people who wear three-inch spike heels to softball practice and eat candy bars for breakfast do the same old tree-trimming, ghost-costume, barbecue, birthday-cake, Easter-egg-hunt thing when it comes to special occasions?

It's probably because these are comforting traditions. But there's a very fine line between comforting tradition and deadly boredom. Should you find yourself dozing off and slumping over that line during some upcoming celebration, remember that the best solution for sameness is strangeness. Then check out the following ideas, presented, where applicable, in calendar order.

EASTER EGGS OF THE RICH AND EVENTUALLY-TO-BE RICH

Kids who wear designer clothes should not be decorating their Easter eggs with stickers and garish Paas pastels. They should marbleize them in the manner of the manors in which they live.

Skins from same number of red or   *Raw eggs*
*   yellow onions as you have eggs*   *Aluminum foil*

Wrap the onion skins around each egg, then wrap in aluminum foil to keep the skins in place. Hard-boil the egg in the usual way (i.e., place in a pot with cold water, bring to a boil, then simmer for about 12 minutes).

An alternate method involves hard-boiling the eggs first, letting them cool, then cracking them all over with the back of a spoon (being careful not to break off any shell). Put the onion skins in a saucepan, lay the cracked eggs on top, and cover with water. Bring to a boil, then simmer for an hour, adding water if it boils away. Cool, peel, and eat.

RITZ MOCK APPLE PIE

There's hardly a recipe in this book that couldn't make a guest protest, "You've got to be kidding." In that sense, almost any recipe here would be appropriate to serve on April Fool's Day. But mock foods are probably MOST appropriate, and readily available between today's ready-to-eat products of science (Sweet 'N Low, Egg Beaters, and Cool Whip) and yesterday's recipes linked to food shortages.

Ritz Mock Apple Pie is an example of the latter. This most famous of all mock recipes is a depression-era reincarnation of a Civil War practice of using hardtack crackers in place of apples, which were available but very expensive.

That doesn't explain why Nabisco received so many phone calls when the recipe was taken off the Ritz cracker box in 1981—when Ritz crackers actually cost more than apples.

Pastry for 2-crust 9-inch pie
36 Ritz crackers, coarsely broken
(about 1¾ cups crumbs)
2 cups sugar
2 teaspoons cream of tartar

2 tablespoons lemon juice
Grated rind of 1 lemon
2 tablespoons margarine
½ teaspoon cinnamon

Preheat the oven to 425° F.

Line a 9-inch pie plate with half the pastry. Place the broken crackers in the crust. In a saucepan, over high heat, bring 2 cups water, the sugar, and cream of tartar to a boil; simmer for 15 minutes. Add the lemon juice and rind; cool.

Pour the syrup over the crackers. Dot with margarine; sprinkle with cinnamon. Roll out the remaining pastry; place over the pie. Trim, seal and flute the edges. Slit the top crust to allow steam to escape. Bake 30 to 35 minutes, or until the crust is crisp and golden. Cool completely. *8 to 10 servings.*

MOCK GOOSE

Here's a place to use the apples you didn't need for the previous mock dish. Of British ration-time origins, it might better fool modern-day Americans if accompanied by many pitchers of beer (and I don't mean mock brands like Sharp's).

*4 to 5 medium potatoes, peeled and
  sliced
2 large apples, sliced
1 cup grated cheddar cheese*

*½ teaspoon dried sage
Salt and pepper to taste
1 14½-ounce can vegetable stock
1 tablespoon flour*

Preheat the oven to 350° F.

Prepare the potatoes, apples, and cheese, then layer them in an ovenproof casserole dish, topping each layer with a sprinkling of sage and ending with a layer of potatoes and cheese. Pour in 1 cup vegetable stock, then bake for 45 minutes.

Remove the casserole from the oven, then pour in the rest of the stock blended with the flour and bake for another 15 minutes. *4 servings.*

MOCK FRIED MUSHROOMS

Yet another use for the much maligned dandelion: to fool. These taste for all the world like fried mushrooms and are as easy to prepare. The fact that the two main ingredients are flower and flour could also provide fodder for some Laurel and Hardy–type kitchen comedy.

*Dandelion flowers
Flour*

Butter

Cut the dandelions at the flower, then rinse in water. Roll the still-damp flowers in the flour. Heat some butter in a frying pan, add the flowers, and fry until brown on all sides. Serve hot.

SILLY SOUP

This is a great centerpiece meal/game for an April Fool's Day or any other potluck. It was undoubtedly inspired by Stone Soup, the French fable about soldiers who trick some stingy townspeople into improving on a "delicious" stone soup by contributing just one bona fide food ingredient each.

1 soup pot
*Meat stock (about twice as much
    as solids you throw in for a
    vegetable-style soup, less for a
    thicker consistency)*

*Anything else anyone wants to throw
    in with the exception of sweets*

Silly Soup is more a concept than a recipe. Anything goes except for sweets. And anyone who contributes must also eat (that eliminates most really awful contributions). It's also good not to add any more than 2 kinds of starches (potatoes and pasta, 2 pastas, etc.).

Cook and stir until all ingredients are done (as little as 1 hour if it contains mainly chopped up vegetables, as much as 4 hours for a Silly Soup containing boar or some other equally tough meat).

ICE CREAM SUNNY-SIDE UP

Pick the birthday of absurdist playwright Samuel Beckett (April 13), or the anniversary of the world premiere of *Betrayal,* a play by Harold Pinter that begins at the end of a couple's relationship and goes backwards from there (November 15), or possibly even April Fool's Day to have a backwards eating day.

Eat dinner foods at breakfast or breakfast foods for dinner. Or go one step weirder and serve a dinner that only LOOKS like breakfast—say, meat loaf baked in muffin tins and savory crepes with gravy poured from a recycled opaque pancake syrup bottle. End the meal with the following simple trompe l'oeil dessert.

½ pint vanilla ice cream   *½ pint orange sherbert or sorbet*

Let the ice cream soften to the point where you can flatten it down onto a small plate into an uneven ¼-inch-thick oval about 3½ inches in diameter. Tidy up the sides, cover lightly with plastic wrap, and refreeze until hard. Make 3 more just like it.

Place half scoops of the sherbert on the center of each ice cream oval so it looks like a sunnyside-up egg. Serve immediately. *4 servings.*

FRIGID WEDDING CAKE
- -

More than half of all the couples who marry in America today will end up splitting up. Here's a wedding cake for people who want to cut down on the expense of the big day, perhaps in anticipation of becoming part of that sad statistic. The recipe is courtesy Sara Lee.

1 sheet of ½-inch plywood cut to exact size of finished cake, 16 inches square, covered with aluminum foil

15 10¾-ounce Sara Lee Pound Cakes, still frozen (they're easier to frost frozen)

4 cups seedless red raspberry jam or spreadable fruit

4 cups unsalted walnuts, ground

6¼ cups white frosting

4 straight candy canes

1 200-square foot roll aluminum foil

4 column cake separators (optional: layers can be set on top of each other)

Silk flowers, ribbons, or pearls for decoration

Stack the pound cakes while still in the boxes and plan your decorating scheme. Remove the cakes from the boxes; save the cardboard lids from all the cakes. Assemble the bottom square tier on the board, using 8 cakes. Cut each cake in half horizontally and spread the bottom half of each with jam; sprinkle each with nuts. Replace the top half of each.

Frost the sides and top of the assembled cake square with a rubber spatula, making 1 large bottom cake tier. Assemble the second tier using 4½ cakes. Do the same thing to them as you did with the cakes in the first tier.

After the top of the second tier is frosted, gently press the 4 candy canes into the second tier in the exact location of the columns. They will give the columns added support. Gently place the columns on the second tier and press into the frosting.

Make the support for the third tier with the cardboard tops from the Sara Lee cake boxes. Stack 3 lids on top of each other and repeat with 3 more immediately next to them. Wrap this "lid platform" tightly in aluminium foil. Stack 6 more lids as before to create a second layer but do not wrap. Place the wrapped layer over the new unwrapped one in the opposite direction (to lend additional strength). Wrap the 2 together tightly with aluminium foil. Repeat for a third layer. Place the "lid platform" on top of the columns.

Assemble the third tier, using 2 cakes. Prepare the layer as before. Assemble the top tier, using half a cake, preparing as with the other layers. Touch up the frosting overall. If a smooth effect is desired, dip a rubber spatula in water and gently move the side of it in one direction over the frosting. Remove any excess frosting the spatula has "dragged" with it.

Decorate with silk flowers, ribbon, pearls, or whatever. Wash the decorations in mild soap and dry thoroughly before using. Be sure to foil-wrap anything that will be inserted into the cake (except the candy canes). *Makes a rectangular 4-layer cake serving 150.*

NOTE: To serve more or fewer people, divide the number of guests by 10 and use that many Sara Lee Pound Cakes.

OLD GLORY CAKE

How did cooking meat become the most popular way to celebrate our nation's birthday? Was it the result of an errant firecracker landing in a pile of charcoal? The invention of some forebear who had meat and a match but no candles and cake?

I suspect the latter. But lest the true meaning of Independence Day fall between the grates of your grill I recommend you make the following bang-up birthday cake for the US of A.

1 18.5-ounce package white cake mix
4 large eggs
1 3-ounce box strawberry gelatin
2 tablespoons flour
¾ cup vegetable oil
1 10-ounce box frozen sliced
  strawberries, with syrup

½ pint fresh blueberries
1 cup whipping cream, whipped until
  stiff
3 tablespoons confectioners' sugar
1 pint fresh strawberries, cut in half

Preheat oven to 350° F.

Mix the cake mix, eggs, ½ cup water, gelatin powder, flour, and oil. Beat together for two minutes at medium speed. Add the thawed boxed strawberries with syrup and about a third of the fresh blueberries and beat another minute. Pour into a greased and floured 13 by 9-inch pan and bake for 45 minutes.

While the cake is cooling, whip the cream and fold in the sugar. Invert the cake onto a platter and frost when cool. Decorate to look like the U.S. flag, placing the remaining blueberries in the left-hand corner and lines of strawberries alternating with lines of plain cream. Refrigerate. Just before serving, further decorate with lit candles or sparklers (where legal) and Pop Rocks popping candy. *10 to 12 servings.*

NOTE: To begin your celebration of the Fourth earlier in the day pour some red- and blue-hued All-American Rice Krispies cereal in a bowl with (white) milk, add some Pop Rocks, and enjoy the fireworks.

POPCORN PIE

Convention and nutrition dictate that a dinner should feature a variety of different foods. That's why breaking those rules in a dramatic way with an all one-food meal can be so much fun.

In-season tomato and zucchini are natural subjects because of the many recipes desperate gardeners have developed for them. You also shouldn't have any trouble coming up with soup-to-nuts meals using popular foods like peanut butter, potatoes, hot dogs, gelatin, garlic, and chocolate.

Since this chapter is for special occasions, I'll suggest doing this on the birthday of someone who loves the food in question, or on the birthday of a food or its inventor.

For instance, an all-popcorn dinner featuring Popcorn Soup (page 71), Movie Theater Lobby Loaf (page 70), and the following recipe for Popcorn Pie (Ruth Pulver's entry in the popcorn cooking contest held in the Orville Redenbacher company town of Valparaiso, Indiana) could be part of a July 16 commemoration of Orville Redenbacher's birthday.

In addition to food, the party could feature horn-rim glasses, costumes, and a corny joke contest.

4 to 5 cups popped Orville Redenbacher's Gourmet Popping Corn (yielding about 3 cups crushed crumbs)	*1 cup sugar*
	½ cup chopped nuts, any variety
	2 cups chunky applesauce
	2 cups whipped cream or topping
3 egg whites	

Preheat the oven to 350° F.

Pop the corn, then crush it, 1 cup at a time, in a blender. Beat the egg whites until stiff, adding the sugar gradually. Add the nuts and popcorn crumbs and spread into a buttered pie plate. Bake for 15 minutes. Cool.

Combine the applesauce with the whipped topping and pile into the cooled crust. Dot with additional topping and refrigerate until serving time. *8 servings.*

HAND-Y HALLOWEEN PUNCH

Only little kids eat candy on Halloween. Today's immature baby boomer adult wants something more imaginative and scary to imbibe on the holiday—such as Hand-y Halloween Punch.

1 package Berry Blue Kool-Aid, unsweetened
½ gallon lemonade or 2-litre bottle citrus soda

One or more pairs latex gloves
Gummi worms

Prepare Kool-Aid according to package directions. Mix the Kool-Aid and lemonade or citrus soda in a punch bowl to create an eerie glowing green drink. Fill the latex gloves with the same mixture, then tie the wrist end closed, allowing some room for expansion. Freeze. Float the gloves in the punch. Decorate the edges of the bowl with gummi worms. *16 servings.*

BLACK JELL-O

Here is yet another Halloween party recipe that proves the value of those high school art class color charts.

1 3-ounce package Orange Jell-O　　　Gummi spiders
1 3-ounce package Grape Jell-O　　　Cool Whip

Prepare the Jell-O according to package directions, then mix together and chill. Decorate with gummi spiders and serve with Cool Whip. *8 servings.*

FOUR-LEGGED TURKEY

This is a fowl trick that will seem like a treat if you have many drumstick lovers at your Thanksgiving table.

1 whole turkey

2 extra turkey drumsticks, approximately the same size of those on the turkey

Before putting the turkey in the oven, cut off both wings with a sharp knife, leaving behind as much skin as possible to help hide what you're about to do. Take the thick end of one of the extra drumsticks and place it in the hole left by one of the wings.

Using a needle and thread (poultry or regular), sew the leg onto the wing socket, trying to let as little thread as possible show on the outside. Repeat with the other drumstick. Roast the bird as usual, then serve.

TRULY DRESSED TURKEY

Thanksgiving turkeys you buy in supermarkets and butcher shops almost always come already dressed in the sense that they are preplucked and ready for cooking. But even turkeys with drumsticks adorned with paper ruffles are not dressed up to the extent of most Thanksgiving guests.

Jim Fobel and Jim Boleach set out to correct this troubling inequity by dressing a turkey with a pastry vest. This is my interpretation of their idea (which first appeared in the food chapter of their *The Stencil Book*), with thanks to Al Sicherman of the *Minneapolis Tribune* for writing about it.

1 10-ounce box 2-crust piecrust mix	*1 egg yolk*
1 12-pound turkey	*Red, blue, and green food coloring*

Make the piecrust dough according to package instructions. Form the dough into a flattened ball, wrap in wax paper, and refrigerate.

Prepare and roast the turkey as usual with 2 exceptions: 1. Make sure to tie the legs together with string, tucking the wing tips underneath. 2. Move the oven rack so there is at least a 1-½-inch clearance between the top of the turkey and the oven ceiling.

Cut a large brown grocery bag into a rectangle 10 x 14 inches (12 x 17 for an 18-pound turkey). Draw a line down the middle vertically, then draw a vest that mirrors itself exactly on each side of the line. (The picture should basically look like a shirt with half sleeves and a V shape at the neck and hips.)

Cut the vest out with scissors. About an 1½ hours before the turkey is due to be done, roll out the piecrust on floured wax paper to an ⅛-inch thickness and a bit larger than the dimensions of your brown bag vest. Lay the vest paper on the dough and trace the shape out with a butter knife. Remove the excess dough and figure out something else to do with it.

Mix the egg yolk with a little bit of water and divide the mixture into 4 muffin tins. Add drops of different food coloring to each tin until the colors are quite strong. Then paint buttons, stripes, and whatever else you like on the vest with a brand-new paintbrush.

When finished decorating, pick up the pastry vest by the wax paper, place on a cookie sheet, and put in the refrigerator until the turkey is about 15 minutes from being ready. Remove the turkey from the oven and raise the temperature to 425° F. Either alone or (preferably) with your turkey assistant, remove the pastry from the wax paper and place it on the turkey (the bottom of the vest should be next to the drumsticks), trimming any excess dough on the sides, if necessary.

Put the turkey back in the oven and bake for 15 minutes, or until the pastry is crisp and the edges are golden brown. *12 to 15 servings.*

THANKSGIVING STUFFED PUMPKIN

The current view of pumpkin as only something to carve at Halloween or cut up to make bread or pie is narrow and recent. For Native Americans and the colonists that copied them, pumpkins were foodstuff, baking vessel, and serving container in one convenient, all-natural package.

Many of the surviving stuffed pumpkin recipes are for desserts that resemble a pumpkin pie filling; others are for stews featuring venison or buffalo meat. But when I heard Native American and pumpkin, I immediately thought Thanksgiving and cooked up this no-fuss, all-in-one, stewlike stuffed pumpkin version of the traditional harvest feast.

1 6- to 7-pound squat-shaped pumpkin
1 cup cooked wild rice
1 medium onion, minced
½ pound sweet Italian sausage, diced
1½ pounds ground turkey

1 cup packaged corn bread stuffing, prepared according to package directions
2 eggs, slightly beaten
¼ cup dried sweetened cranberries
1½ teaspoons poultry seasoning or mixed sage and thyme

Preheat oven to 350° F.

Cut off the top of the pumpkin and clean out the seeds and pulp. Prepare the rice. In a large saucepan, sauté the onion and sausage on the stovetop (use a bit of oil if the sausage isn't fatty enough). Add the ground turkey and brown. In a large bowl, combine all the ingredients, then put into the pumpkin. Replace the pumpkin lid, then put the pumpkin in a baking pan containing about an inch of water.

Bake between 1 and 2 hours, or until the pumpkin seems tender (test by inserting a toothpick in the side—it should go in easily). Don't overcook or it could collapse. Put the pumpkin on a big plate on the table and scoop out or cut out wedges of the pumpkin with the meat mixture as you serve it. *4 to 6 servings.*

WHITE CASTLE HAMBURGER STUFFING

This is one of the first and still one of the weirdest of White Castle hamburger recipes.

10 White Castle hamburgers, cooked
   (if frozen) and with pickle removed
1½ cups diced celery
1¼ teaspoons ground thyme

1½ teaspoons ground sage
¾ teaspoon coarsely ground black
   pepper
¼ cup chicken broth

In a large mixing bowl, tear the White Castle hamburgers into pieces and add the diced celery and seasonings. Toss and add the chicken broth. Toss well. Stuff the cavity of the turkey just before roasting. *Makes 9 cups or enough to stuff a 10- to 12-pound turkey.*

NOTE: For bigger or smaller turkeys, allow 1 White Castle hamburger for each pound of turkey (equivalent to ¾ cup of stuffing per pound).

BRUEGGER BAGEL STUFFING

Just because some people's ancestors came from England doesn't mean the rest of us have to keep making that same old boring white bread stuffing. This Eastern European stuffing inspiration is from Bruegger's Bagel restaurant chain.

3 fresh Bruegger's bagels, any flavor, cut into cubes or ½-inch coins
1 tablespoon olive oil
1 medium yellow onion, chopped
1 celery stalk, chopped
⅛ cup chopped fresh parsley
½ cup low-fat vegetable oil spread or margarine
Salt and pepper to taste
½ cup (or less) water or chicken stock

Preheat the oven to 375° F.

Place the bagel pieces on a foil-lined baking sheet and bake for 15 minutes. Heat the olive oil in a skillet over medium heat and add the onion, sautéing for about 1 minute. Add the celery and sauté until tender. Mix in the parsley. Add the vegetable oil spread or margarine and heat until melted. Add the salt and pepper.

In a large bowl, toss the bagel pieces with the veggie mixture. Sprinkle with the water or chicken stock—enough to get a loose dressing. Stuff and roast the bird immediately. *Stuffs one 10- to 12-pound bird.*

PRETZEL NATIVITY

Here's a new "twist" on the holiday tradition of gingerbread house making: a nativity scene fashioned entirely from pretzels. The instructions—and the idea—is courtesy pretzel maker The Bachman Company.

Assortment of different-shaped
    Bachman pretzels, including rods
    (thick sticks), Stix, Nutzels
    (nuggets), twists, Petites (miniature
    pretzel twists), logs, and sourdough
    hard

Nontoxic, fast-drying craft glue

Begin by building the manger out of rods and Stix. Glue 3 rods together end-to-end to form the triangular base of the roof. Add a rod to each corner to form the legs of the manger and connect with additional side rods. Let dry. Stand the manger on its legs to add a roof. Use 3 rods to make the peak and line with Stix to enclose.

Make people using different-length rod pieces for the bodies and Nutzels for the heads. Use twists broken into C-shaped pieces for the arms. Create an angel by making wings out of 2 Petites, wise men's gifts out of Nutzels, and a shepherd's staff out of a Stix.

Use the knot of 2 twists for the ends of the crib and connect them with Stix. Make sheep by scraping the outside layer off 2-inch pieces of rods. Glue half a Nutzel to one end for the head and use small pieces of Stix for the legs.

To make camels, glue 2 sourdough pretzels together to form the body. Use pieces of rods to make the legs (in either standing or kneeling positions) and the necks. Use a Nutzel for the heads.

To make a palm tree, use a rod as the trunk and glue Stix to the top of it in an inverted umbrella shape. Glue the trunk of the tree to a cardboard base.

NOTE: If you follow Bachman's suggestion of joining pretzel pieces together with craft glue, your nativity scene should obviously not be eaten. To make it edible, use meringue powder icing in place of the craft glue. To make the icing, mix 1 pound confectioners' sugar with 3 tablespoons meringue powder and 6 to 8 tablespoons warm water with an electric mixer at low speed until the mixture is stiff enough to hold a peak but not so stiff that it won't flow through a decorating bag tip.

BEAT THE EGGS, THE CLOCK,
AND THE OTHER COOKS DINNER

Forget gourmet cooking clubs. The best way to have fun around food is to play a home version of the popular BBC-TV show, "Ready, Steady, Cook," or the stateside TV Food Network clone, "Ready . . . Set . . . Cook!" Both shows pit highly regarded chefs against one another in a timed race to create something edible out of a presented pile of ingredients—sans cookbooks or crib sheets.

The results can be pretty amusing with professionals at the helm—imagine how much more so should you invite two teams of rank amateurs to your house on the same pretext. Buy the ingredients yourself or assign the guests to bring specific foods or foods of a certain type (meat or fish, a vegetable, a starch). In the latter case, all the host need do is supply direction, drinks, dessert, and possibly a salad.

Here's one list of possible ingredients to get the party started.

1 pound boneless chicken breast	*6-ounce box stuffing mix*
1 pound bay scallops	*1 piece fresh ginger*
3 tomatoes	*½ pound green beans*
1 8-ounce can chopped walnuts	*1 bunch arugula*
1 3¼-ounce can olives	*1 set of dice*
5 potatoes	*1 timer*
3 peaches	*1 well-stocked kitchen*

Split the party into 2 teams. Have someone from each team roll the dice to see who gets the first ingredient pick (potatoes and peaches go one at a time, bunches of things like green beans go together). Continue rolling the dice until all the ingredients have been picked. Then allow a time for trading (either consensual or dice determined). Contestants should also be given access to all the kitchen basics: flour, milk, butter, eggs, and spices. Set the timer for 40 minutes (longer for less experienced chefs) and let them go.

Everyone tastes each finished dish and votes on the winner—unless it's a particularly cutthroat group. Then get an impartial person do it. *6 to 8 servings.*

"CAN"-YOU-REALLY-BE-THAT-OLD BIRTHDAY CASSEROLE

I ts excessive convenience makes the following recipe for nine-can casserole worth making in and of itself. But it could also be the centerpiece of a birthday party where all the food and gifts are themed to the birthday person's age (or some derivative thereof).

Following those guidelines, nine-can casserole could work for someone turning nine, forty-five or eighty-one. For other ages, add or cut a few cans.

2 5-ounce cans boned chicken	*1 8-ounce can mushrooms, drained*
1 10.5-ounce can condensed cream of	*1 5-ounce can chow mein noodles*
mushroom soup	*1 13-ounce can evaporated milk*
1 10.5-ounce can condensed chicken	*1 8-ounce can water chestnuts*
with rice soup	*1 3-ounce can fried onion rings*

Preheat the oven to 350° F.

Open all the cans. Gather the guests in the kitchen to watch as you empty and mix the contents of the first 8 cans into a 3-quart casserole dish. Bake 40 minutes, then sprinkle on the onion rings and bake another 15 to 20 minutes. *6 to 8 servings.*

GUZZLE-DOWN DRINK

Living in civilized society so often means suppressing natural urges and functions: covering when you cough, stopping a sneeze, using knives and forks when you eat.

Why not break out with a no-utensils dinner party? Pretend you're a Viking—put out some primitive food like ribs, big chunks of bread and cheese, and big steins of grog—a recipe for which is offered below. Then slobber, slurp, belch, and brag. There, now, doesn't that feel better?

1 lemon
2 ounces rum (1 large jigger)

2 teaspoons sugar

Squeeze the juice from half a lemon into a stein; cut a slice from the other half and set aside. Stir in the rum and sugar then fill the rest of the stein with boiling water. Float the lemon slice on top. *1 large serving.*

9

READY-TO-EAT

The number of people interested in strange foods who are also accomplished chefs is probably small. (In fact, if you know of any, could you do me a favor and ask them if they'd like to buy this book?) Subtract from that the number of people who have time to do anything more than call Domino's at dinnertime and the need for a chapter of weird foods that are weird from the get-go becomes clear.

These pre-packaged goodies run the gamut from the deliberately unusual (the gross-out kids' candies) to the unself-consciously strange (dehydrated salsa and the hypodermic needle baster) to ready-to-eats that might just SEEM foreign to good old garden variety, Cheez Whiz eatin' Americans.

ANIMAL EXCREMENT COFFEE

Available from J. Martinez & Company, Atlanta, GA., to those who can afford the price.

In Sumatra, a foxlike animal called the luwak produces the world's most expensive coffee—and excrement. He does this by stealing into coffee plantations late at night, eating the finest coffee berries, digesting them, and leaving nondigestible parts of them behind as droppings.

Gathered, washed, parched, hulled, and roasted, this waste matter becomes luwak coffee, described as "superb" by *National Geographic* magazine. At $300 a pound, it had darn well better be.

GREEN TEA CHOCOLATE BAR

Available in health food stores as Tropical Source Organic Green Tea Crisp for about $2.39 per bar. Made by Cloud Nine, Inc., Hoboken, NJ.

Imagine eating perfumed soap. This Japanese idea seems to have gotten lost in the American translation.

SEAWEED SNACK CAKE

Available at health food stores as Maine Coast Crunch for about $1. Made by Maine Coast Sea Vegetables, Franklin, ME.

Rice Krispies Treats for natural foodies.

SEX SODA

Available in New Orleans, Louisville, Seattle, Houston, Los Angeles, Memphis, Baltimore, San Antonio, Colorado Springs, Winston-Salem, Phoenix, and Washington, DC supermarkets as the fruity Josta from Pepsi-Cola and in thirteen northeast seaboard states as a ginger ale–like Guarana Antarctica from Penguin Beverages, Inc., of Miami, FL.

This soda flavored with the extract of the Amazonian jungle berry guarana is popular in Brazil and in the U.S. cities where it is starting to be introduced. And no wonder. Guarana is widely believed to be a sexual stimulant. (Could it be because guarana also has twice the caffeine of a coffee bean?)

So skip the expensive meal, flowers, and candy and just serve the object of your desire a can of this stuff.

PMS CANDY MIX

PMS Crunch by Time of the Month, Scarsdale, NY is available for $8 a can from Funny Side Up catalog, North Wales, PA.

Considering that many physicians recommend that women with premenstrual problems eat little or no sugar or caffeine-containing foods such as chocolate right before their periods, the physiological soundness of a snack mix containing, as the labels explain, "chocolate, pretzels and more chocolate" or "chocolate, nuts and more chocolate," is somewhat questionable. They are obviously going for the psychological angle (i.e., chocolate's ability to alleviate bitchiness).

PICKLED PIGS FEET

Available in supermarkets nationally for about $1.80 per nine-ounce jar from Hormel, Austin, MN, and other meat product companies.

The worst thing is not the taste; it's that they really look like pig's feet.

CAN O' PORK BRAINS

Available in supermarkets nationally for about 65 cents as Armour Star Pork Brains with Gravy from Dial Corp., Phoenix, AZ.

Sara Lee brownies have gone the way of the Edsel while this is widely available. If that isn't a reason to think America is screwed up, I don't know what is.

FOAM-AT-THE-MOUTH CANDY

Sold under such brand names (and concepts) as Spew, Pond Scum, and Mad Dawg. Available at many novelty candy counters.

Give your next temper tantrum some visual impact by popping some of this foaming candy in your mouth first.

MOCK NASAL DISCHARGE CANDY

Sold at many novelty candy counters as SNOT (for Super Nauseating Obnoxious Treat).

A plastic nose filled with 3.5 ounces of edible drippy goo that's supposed to look like you-know-what. If you're nine years old, this is almost as amusing as knowing a kid who enjoys the real thing.

INSECT LOLLIPOPS

Tequila Worm Sucker and Cricket Lick-It cost $3.95 for three from Archie McPhee catalog company, Seattle, WA.

One nonalcoholic tequila-flavored lolly contains a worm; another crème-de-menthe-flavored one has a cricket. Both are see-through, FDA approved, and healthy because they're sugar-free!

FLAVORED BEETLE LARVAE

A set of twelve, 2½ -inch packets containing thirty-five larvae, called Larvets, costs $13.95. From Archie McPhee.

Weight watchers with strong stomachs will want to try these barbecue, cheddar cheese or Mexican spice-flavored real beetle larvae snacks. Why? Because you probably won't be tempted to eat them and even if you do, they contain less than one calorie each!

BODY PARTS GELATIN DESSERTS

These cost $10 from Funny Side Up.

Catalog companies won't sell you the desserts but they will sell you slightly larger-than-life-sized brain, heart, or hand gelatin molds with recipes for creating realistically colored edible replicas of these body parts. Perfect for Halloween parties, medical school graduation celebrations, and cannibalism cessation programs.

SELF-COOKING DINNER

Available in six varieties for about $5 each at truck stops, sporting goods stores, or directly from HeaterMeals, Inc., Cincinnati, OH.

Talk about your complete meals: These TV dinners come with ¾ pound of food, napkin, fork, salt and pepper, and a packet of water which combines with salt to activate its built-in magnesium-iron alloy "oven."

The technology was previously used mainly for military field rations—a fact the HeaterMeals company would be wise to keep under its helmet.

TOFU TURKEY

Seasonally available in West Coast health food stores as Tofurky or directly from manufacturer Turtle Island Foods, Hood River, OR, for about $50 per six-pound package serving eight vegetarian fanatics.

You might be able to pacify the lone vegetarian at the Thanksgiving table with extra-large servings of vegetables but if the vegetarians outnumber the meat eaters, Tofurky might be the only way your Thanksgiving meal will fly.

It consists of stuffing, gravy, a two-pound turkey-flavored "white meat" tofu roast, and eight "dark meat" tempeh (i.e., moldy tofu) drumsticks. In other words, it's politically but not anatomically correct.

BOILED PEANUTS

Available at Southern roadside stands and by mail order from Lee Bros. Boiled Peanuts Catalogue, Charleston, SC. (800-BOIL-NUT) for $11.25 per 2.5-pound gunny sack.

Roasted peanuts taste like the peanuts most people know and love from peanut butter, peanut butter cookies, Thai dipping sauce, and Planters snacks. Southern-style boiled (unroasted) peanuts taste more like some bizarre combination of hay, barley, chamomile and chestnuts—in other words, nothing like peanuts.

SLIME-FREE OKRA PICKLES

Available in Southern supermarkets from Lee Bros. Boiled Peanuts or directly from manufacturer Talk O' Texas, San Angelo, TX.

Is there any food on earth as vile as boiled okra? But fans of this Texas okra favorite says pickling leaves okra crisp and delicious. I'll let you try it first.

MICROWAVE POPCORN ON-THE-COB

Available as Melissa's Microwave Popcorn Ears for $1.50 to $4 in some supermarkets or by mail order from manufacturer Melissa's/World Produce, Los Angeles, CA (800-588-0151).

An odd combination of the colonial era and the space age—husk-dried corn that can be popped on the cob in the microwave.

DEHYDRATED SALSA

Available in supermarkets as Don Enrique Pronto Salsa for $2.50 to $6 per ¾-ounce bag or directly from manufacturer Melissa's/World Produce.

Lightweight little bag of dehydrated tomatoes, onions, and jalapeños perfect for those who can't think of a better way to end a grueling hike than boiling water to make a nice hot bowl of instant vegetable soup.

SHOOTING UP, CHICKEN ADDICT STYLE

Available in select supermarkets and department stores or directly from The Cajun Injector, Clinton, LA.

A lot of people complain how hard it is to get flavoring into meat and chicken. But Maurice and Edgar Williams did something about it. They created a line of marinades packaged with syringes. Their slogan? "Shoot it, don't soak it."

If only this technique could be used to get information into inattentive schoolkids.

DANDELION COFFEE

Available as Instant Dandylion Blend for about $6 a jar from Goosefoot Acres, Cleveland, OH (800-697-4858).

A caffeine-free alternative to Maxwell House made from the roots of this bane of the suburban lawn ranger. As mail order supplier and dandelion defender Peter Gail says, "If you can't beat 'em, eat 'em."

GRILLED STEAK AND ONION POTATO CHIPS

Available in grocery stores and vending machines for about $1.50 per six-ounce bag and made by Snyder's of Hanover, Hanover, PA.

Traditionally potato chips are served as accompaniments to steak and other sandwiches. But Snyder's of Hanover means to make chips the only thing you need to eat.

In addition to the above-mentioned grilled steak & onion, they offer potato chips flavored like BBQ ribs, buffalo chicken wings, bacon, sausage pizza, and kosher dill pickles.

SMOKED CANNED EEL FILLETS

Available in Asian groceries for about $2 per 3.66-oz. can. Smoked, salted, and packed in oil, eel looks and tastes no worse than sardines. But I get the feeling even Oreo cookies would taste like sardines if smoked, salted, and packed with oil.

DURIAN

Available in Asian grocery stores fresh or frozen for about $8 a pound. A Southeast Asian fruit with a taste so exquisite that one European explorer of the 1700s claimed it alone was worth his journey. It's also supposedly an aphrodisiac. Unfortunately its pulp has the shape and consistency of brain and its smell is so bad that rental cars in Malaysia reportedly bear "No Durian" stickers (similar to the no smoking signs we might see here). Its smell has in fact been compared to sewage or rotting flesh.

In short, durian is the pain/pleasure principle personified.

FIREBALL CANDY SODA

Available as The Grim Reaper for about $1 per twelve-ounce bottle at convenience stores in New England, Seattle, and Los Angeles or directly from the NetherWorld Beverage division of Original American Beverages, LLC., Stonington, CT, or as Brain Wash for $3 a bottle from Brainstorms catalog, Skokie, IL.

New age sodas that require drinking something else to cool your mouth off. The Brain Wash brand also reportedly turns tongues and body waste purple.

STINKING SPICE

Asafetida powder costs about $4 per four-ounce jar from Indian grocery stores or by mail order from Little India Store, New York, NY.

A spice used in many Indian dishes that smells like old gym clothes. It ain't for nothin' that the word *fetid* is embedded in its name.

CAFFEINATED WATER

Sold under the names Aqua Java or Edge2O in California, Aqua Buzz in Denver, Java Johnny in Michigan, Krank2O in Massachusetts, or as Water Joe Caffeine Enhanced Natural Artesian Water nationwide for 89 cents to $1.50 per half-liter bottle, or by the case directly from Water Joe manufacturer Johnny Beverage, Inc., of Chicago, IL (800-862-1066).

The water the docs say we should drink each day plus your gotta-stay-up-all-night caffeine fix all in one upscale package.

EMU JERKY

Emu steak nuggets and pepperoni sticks can be purchased for $1.99 per one-ounce package from BK Emu Products, Turner, OR.

Making meat snacks from this flightless Australian bird sounds may at first sound like a jerky idea. But sales of jerky have risen 15 percent in the United States in the past few years. This is mainly due to Americans' inability to sit down for five minutes even to eat a hamburger, jerky meat's fine nutritional numbers, and the use of such innovative new bases as chicken, turkey, buffalo, venison, and emu (which tastes a lot like venison).

LAXATIVE TEA

Correctol Herbal Tea Laxative comes in cinnamon spice and honey lemon flavors and is available in drug and grocery stores for $4 to $5 per box of fifteen tea bags.

Their slogan is: "Relief for your body. Comfort for your soul." This tea method of delivering Correctol medication will not provide a shield from the shame of having an irregularity problem—not with tea bag tags that scream Correctol Herbal Tea Laxative.

BLACK BREAD SPREAD

Sold under the brand names Vegemite and Marmite for about $6 per 250-gram jar at British food import stores.

The national bread spread of Australia and New Zealand is a yeast extract that looks like tar and tastes like a cross between soy sauce, mincemeat, and licorice. Look no further for the source of the down unders' famed travel lust.

EDIBLE CANDY HOLOGRAMS

Available at convenience and drug stores for 89 cents each or directly from Edible What? Candy, a division of Enviropro International, Richmond Hill, Ontario, Canada.

Thirteen candies that depict three-dimensional pictures when looked at in just the right light. Our favorites are the Action Eats sub-line, which show a bike doing a wheelie, a volleyball player diving for a return, and a baseball player hitting a ball.

What we want to know is: in the darkness of the stomach, do the calories also disappear?

WORM MARGARITA

Mezcal tequila is available in liquor stores for about $5.50 per 200-milliliter bottle.

Mexican liquor derived from the fermented juice of the agave cactus and containing a worm that inhabits it. You're supposed to eat the worm, and if you drink enough tequila you may be able to.

HERBS AND FLOWERS ICE CREAM

Available in many gourmet and specialty food stores across the country or by express mail on dry ice directly from manufacturer Out of a Flower, Dallas, TX (800-743-4696).

Just when I thought I'd seen every flavor of ice cream along comes Out of a Flower, a Dallas-based company that churns out such exotica as rosemary, French lavender, and tarragon ice cream and, for the calorie-conscious, rose or nasturtium sorbets.

The more conventional of their forty-five flavors include pink grapefruit tarragon, spiced red Zinfandel, or their award-winning strawberry, sweet rosemary, and peppercorn sorbets.

OVALTINE MALT ENERGY COOKIES

Ovaltine Biscuits available for about $2 per five-ounce box from the Vermont Country Store, Manchester Center, VT.

Enjoy the vitamin-enriched goodness of classic Ovaltine in an odd new form that allows you to wash down your Ovaltine with a glass of Ovaltine.

FLOATING GELATIN DRINK

Available in grocery and convenience stores as Orbitz by Clearly Canadian, Vancouver, B.C., Canada, for about $1.29 per bottle or as UFO's Beverage by Daily Juice Products, Verona, PA, for $3.29 per four-pack.

Fruit-flavored drink of Far Eastern origins featuring floating gelatin pieces. A bit disconcerting for everyday drinking but it could have potential as training wheels for novice pill swallowers.

Ingredient Sources

For crickets and earthworms: Try a local bait or pet shop or Armstrong's Cricket Farm, P.O. Box 125, West Monroe, LA 71294 (318) 387-6000

For edible flowers: Try a supermarket or health foods grocery with a large produce department or Diamond Organics, P.O. Box 2159, Freedom, CA 95019 (800) 922-2396

For dandelion greens: Belle of Maine canned dandelion greens, W. S. Wells & Sons, P.O. Box 109, Wilton, ME 04294 (207) 645-3393

For squid: Try a local fish market or Battistella's Seafood, 910 Touro St., New Orleans, LA 70116 (504) 949-2724

For moose, rattlesnake, and rabbit: Native Game Co., 1105 W. Oliver, P.O. Box 1046, Spearfish, SD 57783 (800) 952-6321

For turtle, frog's legs, and alligator: Native Game Co.; Deanie's Sea Foods, 1713 Lake Ave., Metairie, LA 70005 (800) 66-CAJUN; or Bayou-to-Go, P.O. Box 20104, New Orleans, LA 70141 (800) 541-6610

For eel: Try a local fish market, Native Game Co., or Maison Glass Delicacies, 111 E. 58th St., New York, NY 10022 (800) UCALL MG

For seaweed: Try a local natural foods or Asian food store or Maine Seaweed Company, P.O. Box 57, Steuben, ME 04680 (207) 546-2875

For Asian specialties (including bird's nest and rice paper): Oriental Food Market and Cooking School, 2801 W. Howard St., Chicago, IL 60645 (312) 274-2826

For ethnic specialties of all kinds: CMC Company, Box 322, Avalon, NJ 08202 (800) 262-2780

Trademarks

Campbell's and V-8 are registered trademarks of Campbell Soup Company.

Hellmann's is a registered trademark of CPC International, Inc.

Best Foods is a registered trademark of Best Foods-Best Foods/Mueller Co.

Hershey's, Reese's, Reese's Pieces, Reese's Milk Chocolate Peanut Butter Cups, and Skinner are registered trademarks of Hershey Foods Corporation. Recipes for Hershey's Cocoa Chili and Rattlesnake Chili courtesy of the Hershey's Kitchens and reprinted with permission of Hershey Foods Corporation.

7-Up and 7UP are registered trademarks of The Seven-Up Company.

Nabisco, A.1., Planters, Oreos, Ritz, Fig Newtons, Mr. Peanut, Life Savers, and Gummi Savers are registered trademarks of Nabisco Foods Group. SnackWell's is a trademark of Nabisco Brands.

Egg Beaters is a trademark registered by Standard Brands, Inc., and owned by Nabisco, Inc.

Pillsbury, Pillsbury Best, and Bake-Off are registered trademarks of the Pillsbury Company.

Spam is a registered trademark of Hormel Foods Corporation for luncheon meat.

Tabasco is a registered trademark of McIlhenny Co.

Lea & Perrins and Worcestershire Sauce are registered trademarks of Lea & Perrins, Incorporated.

Quaker, Quaker Oats, and Aunt Jemima are registered trademarks of The Quaker Oats Company.

Kellogg's, Kellogg's Corn Flakes, Rice Krispies, Rice Krispies Treats, and Froot Loops are registered trademarks of the Kellogg Company.

Tang, Jell-O, Cool Whip, Grape-Nuts, Post, Kool-Aid, Velveeta and Cheez Whiz are registered trademarks of Kraft Foods, Inc. Kraft is a registered trademark of Kraft USA.

Bisquick, Cheerios, Wheaties, and Gold Medal are registered trademarks of General Mills, Inc.

M&M's and Skittles are registered trademarks of Mars, Incorporated.

Coca-Cola, Coke, and Coca-Cola Classic are registered trademarks of The Coca-Cola Company.

Twinkie and Wonder are trademarks of Continental Baking Company.

Morton is a registered trademark of Morton International, Inc.

White Castle is a registered trademark of White Castle System, Inc. Recipes for White Castle Lasagne and White Castle Hamburger Stuffing copyright 1996 White Castle System, Inc.

Ben & Jerry's Ice Cream is a registered trademark of Ben & Jerry's Homemade, Inc.

Mrs. Fields is a registered trademark of Mrs. Fields, Inc.

Sara Lee is a registered trademark of Sara Lee Corporation.

Stouffer's and Lean Cuisine are registered trademarks of the Stouffer Foods Corp.

Budget Gourmet is a registered trademark of The H. J. Heinz Co.

Celestial Seasonings, Sleepytime, and Lemon Zinger are registered trademarks of Celestial Seasonings, Inc.

Orville Redenbacher's is a registered trademark of Hunt-Wesson, Inc.

Pop Rocks is a trademark of Kraft General Foods, Inc., registered by General Foods Corp.

Gerber is a registered trademark of The Gerber Products Co.

Mahatma, Carolina, River, and Riviana are registered trademarks of Riviana Foods, Inc.

Snyder's of Hanover is a registered trademark of Snyder's of Hanover, Inc.

Sunbeam is a registered trademark of the Sunbeam Corporation.

Baskin-Robbins is a registered trademark of Baskin-Robbins USA Co.

Steve's Homemade Ice Cream is a registered trademark of Steve's Homemade Ice Cream, Inc.

Metamucil and Oil of Olay are registered trademarks of Proctor & Gamble Co.

Lady Clairol is a registered trademark of Clairol, Inc.

Bruegger's is a registered trademark of Bruegger's Corporation. Bruegger's Bagel Stuffing recipe copyright Bruegger's Corporation and used with permission.

Tropical Source is a registered trademark of Cloud Nine, Inc.

Josta is a registered trademark of Pepsi-Cola Co.

Armour Star is a registered trademark of Armour Swift-Eckrich.

Grand Marnier is a registered trademark of Cuisine Perel Corp.

Cointreau is a registered trademark of Cointreau America, Inc.

Nerds is a registered trademark of Willy Wonka Brands.

Melissa's is a registered trademark of Melissa World Variety Produce and World Variety Produce, Inc.

Tootsie Roll is a trademark owned by Tootsie Roll Industries, Inc., and registered by Sweets Company of America, Inc.

Paas is a registered trademark of Schering-Plough Health Care Products.

Gak is a registered trademark of Viacom International, Inc.

Domino's Pizza is a registered trademark of Domino's Pizza, Inc.

SuperPretzel is a registered trademark of J&J Snack Foods Corp.

Gravy Master is a registered trademark of Gravymaster Company, Inc.

Jack In The Box is a registered trademark of FoodMaker Company.